D1266783

The Healer's Art

The Healer's Art

*A New Approach to the
Doctor-Patient Relationship*

ERIC J. CASSELL, M.D.

J. B. Lippincott Company
Philadelphia and New York

The epigraph is from "East Coker" in *Four Quartets* by T. S. Eliot, copyright, 1943, by T. S. Eliot, copyright, 1971, by Esme Valerie Eliot. Reprinted by permission of Harcourt Brace Jovanovich, Inc., and Faber and Faber, Ltd.

The lines from Dylan Thomas in Chapter 7 are from *The Poems of Dylan Thomas*, copyright 1952 by Dylan Thomas, published by New Directions Publishing Corporation; and from *Collected Poems*, published by J. M. Dent & Sons Ltd. They are reprinted by permission of New Directions Publishing Corporation, J. M. Dent & Sons Ltd., and the Trustees for the Copyrights of the late Dylan Thomas.

Parts of the Prologue, Chapter 2, and Chapter 6 are based on articles by Eric J. Cassell in *Commentary*: "Disease as a Way of Life," copyright © 1973 by the American Jewish Committee; "In Sickness and in Health," copyright © 1970 by the American Jewish Committee; and "Death and the Physician," copyright © 1969 by the American Jewish Committee. This material is used by permission of *Commentary*.

The material in Chapter 3 was developed in an article, "Making and Escaping Moral Decisions," published in the Hastings Center Studies, Volume I, No. 2, 1973, by the Institute of Society, Ethics and the Life Sciences.

U.S. Library of Congress Cataloging in Publication Data

Cassell, Eric J   birth date
    The healer's art: a new approach to the doctor-
    patient relationship.

    Bibliography: p.
    Includes index.
    1. Medicine—Philosophy.   2. Medicine and
psychology.   3. Physician and patient.   I. Title.
[DNLM: 1. Physician-patient relations.   W62 C344h]
R723.C43   616'.001   75-38686
ISBN-0-397-01098-2

FOR JOAN CASSELL
Out of love and respect

Contents

Acknowledgments

ONE OF THE most wonderful things about medicine is its continuity. Doctors are trained by other doctors. Each physician, then, is not only himself but is made up of other men, and each teacher becomes a part of his students. I acknowledge that debt to my teachers with pleasure. There have been many. At times the contact was brief but the effect lasting. Some of their names are gone from my memory, but what they taught remains. To three I owe an especially great debt. Dr. Cyril Solomon watched me grow from adolescent to physician and tolerated the burden, teaching me all the time. From him I learned that medicine is devoted to the care of persons and much more. As both a pathologist and an internist he showed that it is possible to lead a double life in medicine in which each part enriches the other. Dr. Ludwig Eichna was my teacher when I was a student and house officer. He was able to communicate the excitement of clinical medicine and the rewards of the pursuit of its excellence. Dr. Walsh McDermott was chairman of the Department of Public Health at Cornell, and I learned the wider view of medicine from him. That I learned much more is clear from the number of times I hear his words coming out of my mouth. He was also willing to let me try both academic medicine and practice side by side.

I am indebted to my colleagues at the Institute for Society, Ethics and the Life Sciences. They, too, opened my eyes and my horizons. In addition, every physician knows that his patients are his teachers and so, if for no other reason, I am in their debt. But it is not an exaggeration to say that at the same time they have given me my life. In like manner, one's students are one's teachers; I happily acknowledge that fact because, next to caring for patients, teaching is my greatest joy.

I also gratefully acknowledge the support of the Robert Wood Johnson Foundation for some of the research discussed in this book.

The burdens of the doctor's profession on his family are a legend. My family has borne that burden as well as any I know and has provided me with happiness and security in the process. My wife taught me to write. She has listened to ideas, provided ideas, criticized and complimented. She has always known the right line of poetry, the right book. She has been so much a part of all this that I no longer know where I leave off and she begins.

The wounded surgeon plies the steel
That questions the distempered part;
Beneath the bleeding hands we feel
The sharp compassion of the healer's art
Resolving the enigma of the fever chart.

T. S. Eliot
Four Quartets

Prologue: A Time for Healing

THIS BOOK IS ABOUT the art of medicine—what it means and the origin of its meanings in the human condition, in history, and in the world around us. It is a book about doctors as healers, apart from their technology and their drugs, and what they can learn from the sick, since making the sick better is the final test of any understanding in medicine.

Many years ago, while in residency training at Bellevue Hospital in New York City, I had a midnight call from the psychiatric ward: an old woman was having difficulty breathing. I found the patient gasping for air, her skin blue from lack of oxygen; she had full-blown pulmonary edema (water in the lungs) resulting from a blood clot in her lung. I sent the nurse for the urgently needed oxygen and drugs, but in those days, because of staff shortages and inexorably slow or inoperative elevators, a critically ill patient on a psychiatric ward in Bellevue at midnight might just as well have been in the East River: the wait for the necessary equipment would be interminable. I stood at the bedside feeling impotent, but the old woman's face and her distress pleaded for help. So I began to talk calmly

13

but incessantly, telling her why she had the tightness in her chest and explaining how the water would slowly recede from her lungs, after which her breathing would begin to ease bit by bit and she would gradually feel much better. To my utter amazement that is precisely what happened. Not only did her fear subside (which would not have surprised me) but the noises in her chest disappeared under my stethoscope, giving objective evidence that the pulmonary edema was, in fact, subsiding. By the time the equipment came, things were already under control and the patient and I felt as though together we had licked the devil.

I was, of course, immensely relieved and pleased, but I didn't know what to make of it. Now, twenty years later, I understand much better what had taken place in the middle of that night. I had felt helpless because none of the things I identified with a doctor's job of curing the sick were available; I had none of the technology which, to me, was essential to being a good doctor. What I didn't know then was that desperation and fear had led me unknowingly to function as a healer, a role traditionally played by physicians as far back as Hippocrates.

Today in our society the word "healing" has become identified with charlatanism and quackery, and doctors no longer think of themselves as healers. Several years ago, while writing an essay on changing patterns of disease in this century, I used the word "healer" and suddenly realized that I had no idea what it really meant. I began to explore the subject and found that reading what was available wasn't much help. Most of the literature either reported on healing ceremonies in other cultures (usually from a markedly ethnocentric viewpoint) or interpreted the function of the healer within a psychoanalytic framework as a sort of unlettered psychotherapist—an assumption that seemed to me a simplification concealing more than it revealed.

It gradually became clear, however, that the form that healing took in each primitive society was intimately related to the central beliefs of that particular culture. Such beliefs are concepts of reality but not necessarily, of course, "the Truth." What would turn out to be the central belief, I wondered, if one were to consider doctors trained in Western scientific medicine in the same manner as healers in other cultures? After all, medicine is so important in our culture as to be almost a subculture.

One day, while I was conducting a public-health seminar on cross-cultural medicine, it suddenly occurred to me that the central belief of our medical subculture was disease! Then it followed that modern concepts of disease are not "the Truth" but simply a useful way of organizing observations of reality. The constructs of disease, as physicians learn them, are as surely a belief system as are the constructs of yin and yang found in classical Chinese medicine. They are ways of organizing and thinking about the amorphous manifestations of illness that patients bring to the doctor. Judging from the results of therapy, our belief system of disease is very successful, but it is not the only way of viewing the sick. The ancient Chinese system must also be quite successful, as evidenced by its durability, although judgments of success vary from culture to culture (there is a certain circularity built into the process).

The discovery that constructs of disease are essentially a belief system was a revelation to me, since it tended to contradict the long, intensive technological training centered around disease that all physicians receive. When examining someone who is ill, every physician is so accustomed to looking for the causative disease that the cause of illness is inevitably confused with the phenomenon of illness itself. But the illness and the disease must really be quite separate entities, since sick people have certain characteristics in common and behave in certain similar ways regardless of whether they are sick with pneumonia or have a fractured leg. Thus it seemed obvious that making the distinction between illness and disease could be extremely useful in helping me understand patients and the role of doctors.

I then realized that there must be a similar distinction between healing and curing. If the sick person indeed presents two distinct aspects of his sickness—the illness and the disease that caused it—the doctor must respond with two separate functions, no matter how closely connected they may be or how the curing function may conceal the healing function. To the doctor who does not distinguish between illness and disease, making a patient with pneumonia better means curing the pneumonia—killing the bacteria, bringing down his fever, enabling him to breathe more easily. Indeed, if the doctor does not do those things, it will be bad news for the patient. But there are other aspects of the illness that the doctor may ignore: the patient may be frightened about what is happening in his body; he may feel cut off from his family and his friends; and he may find himself painfully dependent on other people. Handling those aspects of the patient's pneumonia is also part of the doctor's job, a part of his healing function that can be viewed as entirely separate from his function in curing the pneumonia, even if, in practice, the two functions are interrelated. All too often these days the patient must try to cope with those aspects of his illness himself because his doctor either is unaware of the problems or considers them beyond his competency, since it is likely that he was never trained to deal with them in the first place.

Indeed, since bacterial pneumonia is now so easy to treat, the healing function may well not be too important in such cases. It would seem that the technical success of our era, when doctors can be more effective in curing disease than at any other time in history, has contributed to the disappearance of healing as part of the doctor's manifest function. In my opinion this accounts somewhat for the increasing dissatisfaction with doctors. While pneumonia and other infectious diseases can usually be cured, the diseases of present concern, such as heart disease, cancer, and stroke, offer many examples in which cure is impossible and the healing function becomes of paramount importance.

One of the reasons healing is neglected today is a basic confusion among both laymen and physicians about what the role of medicine is. The rise of modern technological medicine has so closely paralleled the disappearance of the infectious diseases of the past and the fall in infant and childhood mortality that it is generally assumed that doctors and their technology are responsible for the health our society enjoys today. Unfortunately, there is little evidence to support the assumption that the health of a population is primarily a result of its medical services—and much to contradict it. As I shall try to show in Chapter 2, our pattern of disease comes primarily from the way we live, and changes in the disease burden of a society are brought about only by changes in our way of life. Simply stated, your doctor with his great technological power may do wonderful things for you when you have a heart attack, but, in order to have a heart attack, you must first have coronary heart disease. People are healthy not because they became sick and were made better but because they didn't get sick in the first place. But doctors and their technology are so effective and so apparent and the intricacies of disease causation are so inapparent that it is natural to relate what your doctor and his technology did for you when you were sick to what doctors and their technology in general do for disease in general.

What is important here is to realize that we, as a society, have come to associate the doctor and his technology so closely and to attribute such power to the association that we have difficulty in seeing them separately when such a separate view is necessary. Furthermore, as a result of the confusion about what doctors and medical care can do for us, we have come to believe that more doctors and more technology will solve our health problems. Increasingly, in the service of that belief, despite some excellent attempts to change the trend, physicians are trained to practice a technological medicine in which disease is their sole concern and in which technology is their only weapon.

But I hope this book will help to make it clear that such a view of the physician's job is extremely narrow, alienating the doctor from his primary role, the care of the sick. The seeming paradox—that seeing their job exclusively as the curing of disease not only prevents physicians from effectively caring for the sick but also reduces their impact on the health of populations—is no paradox at all but results from a failure to perceive the place and function of concepts of disease in these two different areas of medicine's concern.

I have always led a double life in medicine, and so the perspective of this book comes from two different backgrounds. One is the field of public health. For the past fifteen years I have been a teacher and investigator in public health and preventive medicine. Indeed, it was while doing research on the effects of air pollution that I really became aware of the interaction between society and disease. Lest anyone doubt the power of that interplay, consider the impact of the present environmental movement in reducing the bad effects of pollution on the health of our population—an impact that, I believe, will ultimately be greater than that of all the doctors put together.

The other aspect of this book's perspective comes from the wonderful and exciting experiences I have had in caring for the sick. My entrance into that half of my double life in medicine started much earlier than my work in public health. Scared and awed, I walked into the pathology laboratory of the Jewish Hospital of Brooklyn one Saturday morning when I was fourteen. My job was to clean microscope slides and coverslips, but I would have done anything just to be around doctors, hospitals, and patients, as I have been ever since. Through high school and college I worked in various hospitals, usually as a laboratory technician but doing everything I could con someone into letting me do. (It was easier for a young person to work in hospitals then, especially during wartime.) It is a world I love. I wanted to work in all aspects of medicine—to care for patients and to teach and do research. As my training advanced, I was always told that I would have to settle on one aspect or another—academic medicine or practice—but I am still doing both. Although I am a specialist in internal medicine, I am happy that a good part of my practice consists of entire families for whom I have cared for years.

This book comes from a love of the profession. It saddens me when medicine is in trouble, and I think it is in trouble now. Through the ages practically every book about the profession written by a doctor has alluded in its introduction to the fact that the profession is in trouble. Perhaps this has always been true. More likely it shows that medicine is a profession that can never fully meet the expectations of its patients, since it must change to fit the world around it but at the same time remain stable because its basic concerns are unchanging. It also saddens me to admit that it is not a very happy profession. That, too, is a paradox: despite the many positive attributes of a physician's life—good education; important, meaningful, and intellectually challenging work; high status and good income—physicians do not seem to be as happy as one might expect. This is not only a personal observation but is supported by some hard data. Physicians as a group have a high divorce rate and the highest suicide rate of any profession, as well as very high rates of alcoholism and drug addiction. These distressing facts are generally attributed to overwork and grinding fatigue; indeed, they may be contributing factors, but I would wager that they are not the whole answer. (The facts suggest that a research study should be conducted without bias, preconceptions, and misconceptions to find out why doctors are not content.)

Part of the answer is the discrepancy between what physicians are trained to think is important and what turns out to be important when they start practicing, a dilemma represented by what I call the Chief Resident Syndrome. At the end of three or four years of post-medical-school training, a young physician may become chief resident, a position to which all residents aspire. To the medical students and interns he is a minor deity, and the professor or the Chief of Service looks to him as his right-hand man in the training program. He is the embodiment of modern technological medicine, with a seemingly bright future ahead. But if and when the chief resident goes into practice, he may also go into depression. He finds that he has few patients with monoclonal macroglobulinemia and his need for bundle electrograms is infrequent. He has been betrayed. The "crocks" and "gomers" (patients with uninteresting diseases) of yesterday are now his daily patients. His skill is called on for the common cold, diarrhea, and vaginal infections. All this is well known and has frequently been discussed by physicians. But what is not discussed is what happens when a patient with monoclonal macroglobulinemia does come into the doctor's office. Making the diagnosis is not sufficient; the patient must be cared for, not only for the time of hospitalization but for the months or years of his survival—and so must his spouse and his parents. Furthermore, efforts must be made to minimize the patient's disability, to maximize his function and work capacity, and to handle fear and dread, because when these things are done well, the patient, quite simply, is healthier for a longer time, and when they are done poorly, the patient does poorly. About these aspects of monoclonal macroglobulinemia the former chief resident is probably a rank amateur; dealing with these aspects of the patient's illness was not part of his training, since the so-called "psychological" aspects of illness are generally relegated to the psychiatrists or social workers. The chief resident has not so much found out that there isn't a lot of challenging disease around (because there really is) as he has discovered that his technical skill and knowledge of pathophysiology are not inappropriate but are only a piece of what he needs to know. If he gives up on pathophysiology and depends on charm, intuition, and business sense, he simply becomes a bad doctor.

In other words, the ideal for which the doctor was trained turns out not to exist, as such, in the real world. But the real world cannot be dismissed, as the cynics would have us believe, as a place where all the patients' troubles are colds and the rest "psychological" (in the sense of not real). The simple fact is that our chief resident was trained to a very high level of performance and excellence, but for the real world he is not excellent. He has been given a good start, but he is not excellent. It is possible that such a situation could make a man unhappy. If he stays in practice and doesn't learn for himself how to carry out his healing functions, he will, I believe, accuse himself of having lost his ideals and either stay unhappy or find happiness elsewhere. As is usually the case, we don't find the ideal lacking; we accuse ourselves of failing the ideal.

Don't feel too badly for the chief resident; even if he goes into practice, he often gives it up and returns to the university medical center to teach other young men about medicine (and about how practicing physicians are money-minded or whatever) and so it goes, on into the next generation.

It is necessary to make it very clear that the picture of medicine drawn in this book is not offered as an alternative to technological medicine. No physician in his right mind would want to slow progress or return to a time of lesser diagnostic or therapeutic power. And any doctor who does not keep abreast of new developments and maintain his control of the technology will become its slave. (There is an equal danger, however, that one can become a slave to the technology by embracing unthinkingly the belief system that supports it, even when it begins to evolve past utility.) What I am suggesting is that the balancing force to technology in medicine must be restored. That balance will be found, I believe, by a return to a much wider view of the doctor's job, a view that restores healing to its place alongside curing as a trained and disciplined part of the physician's role.

This goal will not be accomplished by telling doctors what is wrong with them or exhorting them to be good guys. Physicians are not partial to philosophy; they are pragmatists. If they are to change, it will not be because courses in the humanities are added to the curriculum, however desirable that may be, but because they are taught a way that works better. The forces for such change in other segments of our society are growing and cannot help but influence medicine. It is my own deeply personal belief that a return to a more balanced view of the doctor's role will produce not only more effective doctors but also happier doctors.

Finally, a word to those physicians who may find what I have said in this book to be self-evident because they have come to the same conclusions as I have. I hope they will be heartened to realize that someone else understands with them the importance of restoring the art of healing to the medicine of today.

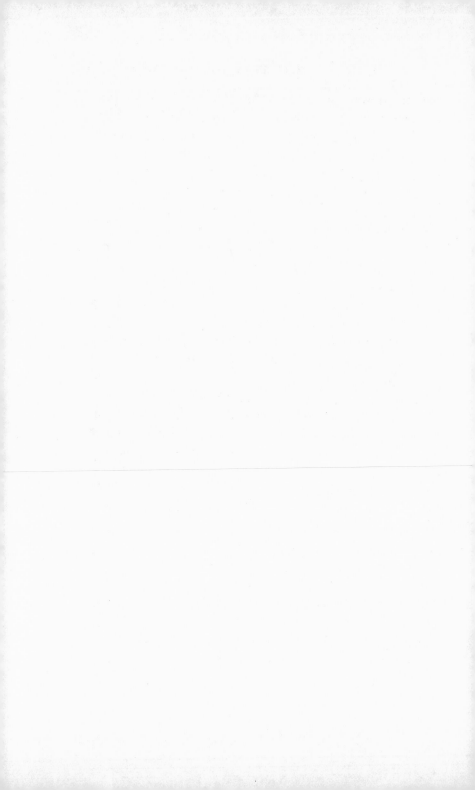

1 The World of the Sick

WITH ITS SIREN cutting a path through the traffic, the ambulance briefly suspends the law against going through a red light. As it slows, people turn to stare at the prone passenger being rushed to the hospital—to another world, a world within our world but separate.

What is sickness to a hospitalized patient? The world around the person shrinks to such a small space, scarcely larger than his own body—the box of tissues on the bed, the bed itself, and perhaps the room. Someone may be nearby but seems not to be there, so faint is the connection to others. The patient becomes disconnected from the world, feeling as if it would be fearfully easy to fall off.

So pervasive is the helplessness that distress, pain, and weakness may appear to be the only realities. Understanding fails and sustained thought seems too difficult to achieve. All control of the world is gone. The button that calls the nurse seems, in the proverbial length of time for a response, an impotent scepter. The bed is made while the patient is moved from side to side, as powerless as a baby being diapered.

The patient is dependent on all around him. A visitor

25

or an attendant thoughtlessly pushes beyond his reach the bedside stand holding his eyeglasses and the water pitcher, thus condemning him to thirst and robbing him of clear vision for hours. The simple everyday rules that govern the way we act are changed for the sick. Though their world and ours look the same, sound the same, are the same, the rules are different, as in a science fiction story in which an alien from another planet invades an earthman's body and takes over. Nobody can tell because to all appearances the earthling is still the same, and thereby hangs the danger.

The word "sick" implies not merely illness—a feeling of unfitness—but a state in which danger to life exists and urgent action is demanded. One cannot be sick without being ill, but sickness apparently has another dimension. One of my patients was a young woman who had had severe poliomyelitis as a child. Paralyzed from the waist down, she went to school through college on her crutches. Despite all the difficulties, she married and worked as a teacher. Over the years back pain had been an increasing problem, until pain and its avoidance gradually became the dominant theme of her life. When severe headache joined the back pain, she went from doctor to doctor without obtaining relief. Then, in her own words, she "started to get sick." Frequently unable to go to work, she remained in bed and, she said, spent most of her time sick. Sickness, then, is something more than illness.

As another example of the difference between illness and sickness, a physician developed an abscess in his abdomen and was admitted to the hospital. His temperature was high and the other signs of the disease and the diagnosis were evident both to him and to the doctor who attended him. Despite considerable pain and discomfort, he and his doctor discussed his problem (which was serious) with the badinage and humor peculiar among physicians. But when his doctor saw him on the following morning, he seemed to have lost interest in the conversation. Both of them became frightened. Before that he had been ill; now he was sick!

In health we know we are alive by our connectedness to the world. When we are totally disconnected, we are dead. We are connected to the world by numerous physical phenomena—touch, sight, balance, smell, taste, hearing—and also by our interest in things and in others, by our feelings for people, by what we do and how necessary we are, by our place in the social scheme. To the degree that we feel real confidence in those connections, small details are unimportant and losing some connections is not so frightening as losing others. In illness, however slight, some of these contacts are lost. Even a bad cold may make it difficult to maintain interest; besides that, the tearing of your eyes may interfere with your vision, but at least you know what is causing the disability and realize that it will soon pass.

As illness deepens, connections are increasingly cut off by the symptoms of sickness and by the forced withdrawal from society caused by sickness. The patient is alternately frightened by the perception of his withdrawal and disinterested in the loss as his horizon shrinks. As he leaves the world of reality, he begins to build a world of his own, an inner world or a world shared exclusively with other sick. Sometimes the new world may be so appealing that return from its simpler delights may be difficult. For the tuberculous patient, for example, the physical and moral disconnectedness traditionally associated with tuberculosis is assumed in our culture, so that Thomas Mann's use of the disease as an allegory in *The Magic*

Mountain can be universally understood. In *The Magic Mountain* a ritual attends the process of joining the new world, and although there is much talk of release from the sanatorium it is clear that its inhabitants are ambivalent about leaving it. Even today, when the treatment of tuberculosis has so changed that usually the patient may quickly resume his normal life, the disease retains its earlier connotations.

One of my patients, a decisions analyst for a think tank, was found to have tuberculosis. I had expected him to be upset at the diagnosis and the necessity of spending a month or so out of circulation. On the contrary, within a few days he was comfortably ensconced in his hospital room, with a whole library of books scattered about. Apparently, he felt that the romantic role of the tuberculous intellectual—so prevalent in the nineteenth century—suited him admirably.

The disconnectedness that occurs with sickness is obviously a complex affair that can occur at many levels. It can be precipitated at a wholly sensory level, demonstrated in experiments on sensory deprivation in which the subject floats weightless in a tank of water, shut off from all the usual visual, tactile, or auditory stimuli. In such experiments the disconnectedness frequently results in hallucinations.

Disconnectedness may occur rapidly in acute illness, as in the aforementioned example of the physican with the abdominal abscess, or more slowly in chronic illness such as tuberculosis. In tuberculosis social forces appear to be more active than physical forces—a situation that is equally true of leprosy, the victims of which have become the proverbial outcasts of society. Disease may also place its victims beyond the moral pale, as exemplified by the reaction still evoked by the venereal diseases despite their now simple treatment. So we see that the range of disconnectedness is as great as the range of connections—physical, emotional, and social—of the individual to his world.

Furthermore, because we are biological, psychological, and social beings, the disconnectedness of illness may not necessarily be imposed by society. For example, it may come, in part, from the refusal of the medical profession to legitimate the illness. A patient suffers for months from an illness characterized by vague joint aches and muscle pains, with occasional bouts of low fever. "A virus," says one doctor. "Probably psychosomatic," says another. "Learn to live with it," others say. During these months the patient knows that something is wrong but becomes increasingly withdrawn because society refuses to grant him the right to what the sociologists call "the sick role."

Because of its many facets, the disconnectedness of sickness is potent. I have begun to think that the word "hopeless" stands for disconnectedness. To have hope is still to feel a connection to the social group, for in that joining we are whole. Just how potent or dangerous is the loss of connectedness is seen in the phenomenon of voodoo death, a process incisively described by the French anthropologist Claude Lévi-Strauss in his *Structural Anthropology:*

> An individual who is aware that he is the object of sorcery is thoroughly convinced that he is doomed according to the most solemn traditions of his group. His friends and relatives share this certainty. From

then on the community withdraws. Standing aloof from the accursed, it treats him not only as though he were already dead but as though he were a source of danger to the entire group. On every occasion and by every action, the social body suggests death to the unfortunate victim who no longer hopes to escape what he considers to be his ineluctable fate. Shortly thereafter social rites are held to dispatch him to the realm of shadows. First brutally torn from all his family and social ties and excluded from all functions and activities through which he experienced self-awareness, then banished by the same forces from the world of the living, the victim yields to the combined effect of intense terror, the sudden total withdrawal of the multiple reference systems provided by the support of the group, and, finally, to the group's decisive reversal in proclaiming him . . . dead and an object of fear, ritual, and taboo. . . . physical integrity cannot withstand the dissolution of the social personality.

Along with his loss of connectedness to the world, the sick person suffers a loss of his sense of indestructibility. When healthy, each of us takes his body for granted and prizes his body image. Even though we may not like its appearance, we value its intactness, its readiness to do and go. However, intelligence tells us what must happen to everyone: this is a hostile world and death is inevitable. Experience is the enemy of comfort and continuity because it portends the surety of death, but our knowledge is no match for the powerful sense of omnipotence in all of us that denies the possibility of destruction.

The feeling of omnipotence must be maintained in the face of a steady attack on its integrity by reality. The importance of a sense of personal indestructibility is easily demonstrated by those who have been involved in automobile accidents. Even though their injuries may be minor, they are shaken for days, and the process of rebuilding their shattered sense of omnipotence may be slow indeed.

Illness threatens the sense of indestructibility, and the threat must be met. One of the familiar defenses is the process of denial—the refusal to recognize that anything is wrong, sometimes in the face of awesome evidence to the contrary. I remember a patient who walked down the hallway of my office with a spread-legged, foot-flopping gait. Sitting opposite me, she repeatedly dropped her cigarette while trying to light it. She had come because of pain in her abdomen. "How long have you walked like that, and how long have you been dropping things?" I asked. "I don't drop things! What do you mean—walk like what?" she asked. Despite her very considerable intelligence, she had managed to deny to herself the terrifying symptoms of what turned out to be a spinal-cord tumor. Another patient with a spinal-cord disease had considerable weakness in his legs, but he walked almost normally until denial failed him. On occasion a patient may report a sudden worsening of symptoms when what has happened is that denial has failed and the hitherto ignored symptoms had to be acknowledged.

The reverse may occur. A hypochondriacal man suffered a heart attack. After the event, rather than becoming increasingly concerned with his symptoms, he altered his entire pattern of activity and fears and succeeded in hiding from himself the extent of his cardiac disability. Several years passed. He came to my office one evening in acute distress that, though not typical, seemed to me to be cardiac in origin. I had not been his physician previously and he did not tell me of the prior heart attack, but I had him admitted to the hospital. The next morning he felt better, and on requestioning and reexamining him I felt somewhat foolish at having been what I thought was falsely alarmed. At this point I suspected that I had been wrong and that the symptoms were instead indicative of disease of the stomach or gallbladder. Tests for these and other possible diseases were negative, and he was discharged from the hospital.

Within a month it all happened again: he had sudden, acute distress that appeared to be cardiac in origin, causing me to hospitalize him. Again, the morning after, I seemed to have been falsely alarmed. However, this time I ordered more diagnostic tests. The fact of having been twice "fooled" by his distress made me think that I had not been fooled at all. In the acute situation his body said one thing; but when the symptoms (and fear) had quieted, his powerful and pervasive denial of heart disease took over again.

Exercise studies and coronary angiography established the diagnosis of coronary heart disease. When the findings were being discussed with him, he was surprised and dismayed: "I've never had trouble with my heart!" His wife, who had been listening to the discussion, was amazed. "What do you mean, Sam? You had a heart attack in 1958!" He said, "You know, Doc, I forgot all about that."

It subsequently turned out that he couldn't walk three blocks without suffering from "indigestion," which was how he accounted for his angina pains. To avoid the problem, he had simply stopped walking.

Certain symptoms are more shattering than others. A vigorously healthy executive in his forties came back from lunch and started talking to his secretary but became aware that the words were not coming out of his mouth properly. (Later his secretary said that he had sounded odd, but she had thought that he was "high.") He decided to go home and went to the bus terminal. As he reached the ticket counter the name of his destination was in his head, but he couldn't make his mouth say it. Frightened, he went to the end of the line again, but on reaching the counter, he was still unable to speak properly. At that point he asked for help. Later, sitting with the police while waiting for his brother, he discovered that he couldn't find his pocket with his hand. He was hospitalized, but the next morning his thinking, speech, and coordination were normal, although he was terribly frightened by what had happened. Extensive neurological testing failed to reveal the cause. Some months later the same symptoms recurred, but this time the tests revealed a brain tumor from which he subsequently died.

Symptoms such as this executive experienced strike at one's sense of self. To understand how devastating such symptoms can be to the sick person's sense of omnipotence, remember (if you have had the experience) how terribly upset you became when you were at the bedside of someone close to you and his mind wandered. As my aged father was dying, I could accept the fact that his body was winding down, but I was struck through with pain and sadness at those moments near the end when he hallucinated. In some cases such symptoms occur so frequently that the physician is able to forewarn the patient and the family and thus ameliorate the impact. Hallucinations are common in the surgical intensive care units where patients are taken after cardiac surgery. Despite having been fore-warned, one of my patients who had artificial valves im-planted said months later that he knew the bizarre inci-dent he had described after surgery could not have oc-curred—it must have been a hallucination—and then added, "But I just know it happened."

Hallucinations or mental aberrations during an ill-ness are extremely disturbing for anyone but especially for an older person. It may be exceedingly difficult to convince such a person that hallucinations during an episode of sickness do not portend the senility dreaded by all of us.

In the sick the loss of the feeling of omnipotence, like the loss of connectedness, can occur socially as well as physically or psychologically. Our omnipotence is threat-ened whenever our social being is invaded by sickness. Think of the overwhelming embarrassment that attends incontinence. I remember a physician who was severely and acutely ill. One of his symptoms was uncontrollable diarrhea. The look of pure anguish on his face was pitiable as he had to be helped to undress and to be cleaned up like a baby. In a similar situation are those, who, because of their disease, are to their fellows foul in sight, smell, or sound.

If you wonder why one needs a sense of omnipotence, a sense of indestructibility, consider whether you could cross a city street without it. Then ask yourself how you ride a bicycle. Most of us don't know how; we just do it. And we don't watch our feet when we walk or dance. We need to soar above our bodies, our everyday thoughts, and our social connections to be whole and to grow. With the loss of the sense of omnipotence this ability disappears and we are crippled.

When we are ill, we not only become disconnected from our world and lose our sense of omnipotence but reason fails us. As Lévi-Strauss has pointed out, normal thought continually strives to understand the universe even though its dynamics cannot be controlled and events refuse to reveal their significance. In illness, too, we attempt to understand, but the disease process is beyond our control and the significance of events is often beyond our knowledge. Because in this instance lack of understanding threatens our completeness and exposes us to unknown dangers, we make new and repeated interpretations with added emotional content to compensate for a deficient reality. Rather than bringing comfort, each new interpretation only shows more clearly the tattered edges of our understanding and more and more emotion fills the thought. Furthermore, it is as though some force directs each new interpretation of symptoms closer to the edge of the abyss. Thus the patient often comes to the doctor with a simple illness to which has been added totally unrelated events, the whole interpreted by the patient as fearful or even fatal disease.

It is very important for us to understand that thought patterns change in the sick. We tend to assume that everybody thinks as we do—not the same thoughts, of course, but in the same way, employing the same processes of reason. It appears not to be true, however, of the sick.

In professional discussions of medical care, the doctor-patient relationship, the behavior of patients, and such ethical issues in medicine as who shall make the decisions, the assumption is often made that the reasoning of the sick is predominantly intellectual, or rational, based on facts and objectively reached concepts. While the sick may think rationally when they are able to consider the presidency or the Constitution, their thoughts about themselves or their illness appear to be primarily emotional. (As we have seen earlier, because of their loss of connectedness to the larger world, the sick tend to lose interest in such matters as politics. For example, it would be unusual for someone who had undergone major surgery to pick up a newspaper until a few days after the operation, and even then it would be difficult for him to sustain interest.)

However else emotive thought may differ from the rational, in emotive thought feeling deeply influences the way in which new information is perceived. Generally, a fact or a piece of information does not float free in our heads; it is assigned to some category or frame of reference that already exists within the mind. Not only is the information assigned to a particular category, but it is given strength or weight within that category. Experience, education, social background, and a host of other factors contribute to the mind's "decision" as to where to assign incoming information. In the sick, feelings such as fear strongly influence this process.

When a patient goes to a doctor and gives the history of his illness, he doesn't usually report a collection of facts he has observed but rather gives interpretations. He may say, "Last week I had a virus and then—remember how it rained on Friday? Well, I got soaked and it settled in my chest." In that very typical "history," the patient has not provided the doctor with a single symptom—a single one of his original alien body sensations.

An experienced nurse and her husband came to see me about the husband's chest pain. In the site of the pain, its character, its relation to physical effort—in virtually every detail—it was typical angina pectoris. After the examination was completed, I discussed the diagnosis with them. They were completely taken by surprise. Heart disease had never occurred to the wife, even though as a nurse she realized, when the facts were reviewed, that it was obvious.

During World War II the husband had been in a tuberculosis sanatorium—the dominant fact of their young marriage. Over the weeks since the pain had started, they thought only of tuberculosis and the probability that he might have to return to a sanatorium. In other words, the meaning of the pain was completely distorted by past experience and fear. Although we have been speaking of the sick throughout, here the wife, who was not ill, shared the husband's emotive interpretation. The case should make the point that the boundaries of illness are poorly defined. In this instance it was not only his person that was threatened by sickness but the marriage—their combined person. Sharing in the illness by spouse or parent is not unique and can seriously mislead the incautious physician. Illness disturbs not only the homeostasis, or vital balance, of the patient but that of the family or even of a wider group. Therefore, others are caught up in the illness process. For example, consider how deeply involved a psychiatrist's patients would be if he or she became seriously ill.

Another example shows how both rational and emotional perceptions of symptoms can exist side by side in a sick person. A woman had a hysterectomy during which the left ureter (the tube from the kidney to the bladder) had been cut by accident. Two years later, she was told that X rays showed the left kidney had atrophied. Subsequently, she reported to me that for several weeks she had felt increasing pain in her left side and upper abdomen. Then she developed a fever and was admitted to the hospital. It was found that the atrophied kidney had been converted to a large cyst that had become infected. Before I gave her the diagnosis, I asked what she thought was the matter. "I know, because all my family has heart trouble, that it must be my heart," she said, and then added, "But when I wasn't frightened, I told my husband that I bet I have a big kidney like a football that's hitting against my ribs."

To understand how sickness can change thinking, one must go beyond the emotive, the effect of preconception, fear, or feeling.

A number of years ago one of my patients had a massive gastric hemorrhage, requiring surgery for its control. Postoperatively, he was in critical condition for a few days. In addition to his other troubles, he was, to quote the nurse, "in and out of his tree"—hallucinating from time to time. On the second day after writing my orders, I returned to the bedside. I kept saying to myself, "If I only knew what you are thinking, Edgar, I would know so much more about sickness and the sick." In one of those rewarding moments of inspiration, I decided to duplicate a famous experiment conceived by the noted French psychologist Jean Piaget. I took two transparent specimen cups and a tall, thin test tube from the sink; filled the test tube with water; emptied it into one of the short, squat cups; and repeated the procedure with the other cup. Both cups now had the same amount of water, and the test tube was empty. I returned to the bedside and showed the cups to the patient. "Edgar," I said, "these two cups contain the same amount of water." When he acknowledged that, I told him to watch as I poured the contents of one of the cups into the test tube. Pointing to the filled test tube and the remaining cup of water, I asked, "Edgar, which one has more water?" To my astonishment, he pointed to the test tube. My middle-aged patient's response to this classic test of reasoning on the conservation of volume was the same as that of a child under six.

I have repeated the demonstration many, many times and have found that the very ill, even when they appear to be in complete possession of their mental faculties, almost always respond in the same way Edgar did. Of great interest is the reaction of a bright twenty-nine-year-old legal secretary, who, because of an unusual kind of heart disease (cardiomyopathy), had been in the hospital for nine months. She was entirely free of symptoms and about to go to a convalescent home. I was prompted to try the test on her because the social worker reported great difficulty in getting the patient's cooperation in working out the ordinary details of her transfer to the other facility. This patient also indicated that the test tube held more water. A year or so later I asked her about it and she said, "I watched you do it and I thought, 'I *know* the test tube can't have more water,' but I looked at it and it did, so I said it." Again, the two kinds of thought existed side by side.

From such evidence, we can conclude that, although we may not understand exactly why, the sick may reason differently from the well. Fear and other feelings all play their part; but further, in serious illness the very processes of thought change. Neither we nor the sick know that their thinking is different; the realization must be denied because it is so frightening.

How difficult it is to accept the failure of reason is

demonstrated by the reaction to the test procedure of a man in his sixties who was having considerable difficulty after gallbladder surgery. He, too, stated that the test tube contained more water, but he seemed somewhat upset afterward. The next day the curtain was drawn around his bed as he talked with a visitor while I was examining the patient in the bed next to his. He did not know of my presence, and I inadvertently overheard him telling the visitor about the test with the containers of water. He explained with distress that he knew that both had to have the same amount of water; nonetheless, he had also known that one container had more. His visitor, taken aback, said, "Harry, you've always been a logical man . . . in sickness and in health you are a logical man."

In health Harry may have been a logical man, but in sickness none of us are.

Thus, to the loss of connectedness and of the sense of omnipotence that occur in sickness, we must add the failure of reason—the loss of the sense of omniscience. There are other characteristics of the sick that will be described shortly, but let us pause for some general observations.

The degree to which these terribly important phenomena occur in the sick varies with the severity of the illness, the personality structure of the patient, the meaning of illness to him, and the setting in which the illness occurs.

The degree of illness is not solely an objective matter. Certainly catastrophies may overtake any of us, quickly plunging us into the world of the sick. Hemorrhage, shock, stroke, severe heart attacks, mangling accidents may, within minutes, transform the healthiest person into a sick one exhibiting all the characteristics that have been, and will be, discussed. On the other hand, the same disease process may affect each person differently. It is the individual's perception of illness that counts, as exemplified in the following two cases.

A postoperative patient developed an extremely dangerous heart rhythm disturbance. It was corrected rapidly with a minimum of fuss, and he experienced almost no untoward symptoms. On leaving the hospital, he said that he was happy not to have had any trouble after his operation.

Another patient, a robust young man, was to have a test done during which allergic reactions sometimes occur. The test room was crowded with oxygen tanks, cardiac monitors, and other resuscitation equipment. The young man asked why the equipment was there and the nurse told him, "Just in case something happens." He had been informed that an allergic reaction was possible, but he deduced the degree of what might "happen" by the array of equipment (which fortunately did not have to be used). Nevertheless, he was scared for days at what he perceived to be his "close call."

The perceptions may be entirely personal, or they may be "borrowed" from others. But by far the most important source that determines our perception of disease is the cultural milieu. As was noted earlier, such diseases as tuberculosis, leprosy, and the venereal diseases have meanings to us that often extend far beyond their physical effects, and their significance in the cultural consciousness does not seem to change even though the treatment of the disease has been drastically altered by technological advances.

In the United States heart attacks have acquired their own mythology. We even feel that we know who is going to get one. "If he keeps on going like that," we say, "he's going to have a heart attack." In our minds, heart attacks have a relationship to what we do, as though we bring them upon ourselves (and, in a complex way, we do, since there is much evidence to indict such personal habits as diet, cigarettes, and lack of exercise as causative factors). But again and again a heart attack is seen as a stopping point, a point at which the patient must take stock of his life. The patient certainly feels that way—"It's all over; I'll never be active again!"—almost as if he hadn't gotten away with "it." He had tried to deny the existence of physical weakness; he had tried to ride through on his sense of omnipotence and had failed. Although many see any physical illness as failure, failure is implied in this disease as in no other—failure in life, a feeling of being cast aside from the mainstream of American life. It is as if all of us were children hanging on the back of a bus, and one fell off. Thus, the man with a heart attack is "out of the rat race." These feelings of failure and depression that so commonly accompany a heart attack occur in the early days of the event. As time passes, denial again gathers force and the negative feelings subside as the breaches in the muscle of the heart and in the sense of omnipotence heal.

We now know that in most instances the survivor can resume normal life, but implied in the resumption is a moderation of life-style. A patient who two years earlier had had a heart attack was stricken with abdominal pain and fainted in his office. The overriding concern was whether he had sustained a second heart attack. Several days of inconclusive tests passed, during which he was immersed in depression. When he finally heard the diagnosis that no second heart attack had occurred, he was immensely happy. "I knew it couldn't be," he said. "I've done everything right since the first one and I knew I couldn't have another." Good behavior offers no such guarantee, but so intimately have we entwined classic American excess with the production of heart attacks that the two are firmly bound in our minds, as though the total comprised the pathological state. Fortunately, the use of exercise as a treatment after heart attacks or as a preventive factor is beginning to change this picture.

No discussion of the importance of the perception of a disease in determining the degree of illness can avoid a discussion of cancer. Cancer is a special case. I do not pretend to understand all its meanings to us, but some things seem clear. Cancer is the enemy within, a cannibalistic enemy. Cancer is personified. My niece has a rat named George with a tumor growing on its leg; she named the tumor Harry!

The word "cancer" strikes dread in the hearts of all. It implies not only death but protracted pain and burdensome illness. The optimism that has come to pervade much of our attitude toward disease in the United States has made little inroad here. Hope is extinguished by the diagnosis of cancer, which has come to stand for the stroke of unjust fate. It shows us how a word can have many meanings. For the individual patient with a specific cancer, it may have little effect if it is one type and great consequences if it is another. The word "cancer" itself, however, carries a cargo of meanings wider than those of any individual case, meanings that comprise the cultural perception of the disease.

Cancer, like tuberculosis, can convey the personal meaning of illness in the world of the well and of the sick. *The Cancer Ward* by Alexander Solzhenitsyn uses the cancer wing of a Soviet hospital as an allegory for authoritarianism, repression, and exile. The universal concept of cancer in the metaphor makes clear the striking effect of illness without hope in removing man from control of his own life. Cast into the hospital world of doctors and nurses, the individual is impotent in the face of the medical array because he needs it to maintain the hope of survival. Dignity is a luxury of the healthy, and self-respect requires a constant struggle. Control in this other world is in the hands of others. The sharpness of the line that divides the worlds is made clear in the book when the head radiologist, having too long concealed her symptoms, is X-rayed and presumed to have cancer. Although we strongly suspect it, we are never told whether she does or not; it is unimportant. She no longer X-rays; she is X-rayed. The sick do not do; they have done to them.

To the other characteristics that distinguish the sick from the well we must add the loss of control over the world. Not only may the facts of the illness, such as the inability to run one's business, destroy control but the inactivity and confinement may be similarly destructive. Some of us use the very fact of our physical activity as one of the ways we run our world. To such people the bed is anathema; the very inactivity itself plunges them more deeply into illness. If I had to pick the aspect of illness that is most destructive to the sick, I would choose the loss of control. Maintaining control over oneself is so vital to all of us that one might see all the other phenomena of illness as doing harm not only in their own right but doubly so as they reinforce the sick person's perception that he is no longer in control.

Thus, to a degree that varies with the severity of the illness or the perception of its severity, tempered by personal experience and the cultural milieu, the sick person becomes disconnected from the world, experiences a loss of the sense of omnipotence and a failure of reason, and loses control over his own existence. We have seen that these elements of sickness can be determined as much by cultural as by physical or emotional factors. Creating such a division into physical, emotional, and cultural modes is, of course, an artifact of discussion necessary for clarity, for no such sharp lines separate them within ourselves. Nonetheless, such a separation should make clear that discussing illness in only physical terms (or even in purely psychological terms, which has become popular today) leaves out the essential dimensions that characterize the sick as well as the healthy.

There is one time in our lives, common to us all, when we are in a state of helplessness: infancy. The infant has a muddled nervous system, a seeming inability to communicate, a tiny world, and useless appendages. Infancy is a frightening state—if not to the infant, then in retrospect. The sick have much in common with the infant. The significance of this comparison becomes apparent when one sees the face of someone who is clear-minded but very sick as he lies surrounded by the smelly mess of his illness. And yet I have avoided the word "regression" in discussing sickness. The word hides more than it describes.

When told how my patients reacted to Piaget's test for the conservation of volume, one of my friends said, "Well, that's regression." He is right, but it gives regression a deeper meaning than I ever dreamed it had.

Similarly, in describing the sick I have avoided using the word "dependent" for several reasons. It is perfectly apparent that the sick person is dependent. But the word, while it may comprise the elements I have described, contains neither their force nor their separate meanings. Furthermore, dependency, as we use it, is not entirely a bad state. It is necessary to be dependent to be a social animal. It has within its meanings the ability to receive what others give—the ability to be loved. Therefore, when we say that the sick are dependent, we say they are takers of what others give. It is that part of the state of illness that is openly desirable. It is that part of the state of illness that clearly offers enrichment to those around the ill. It is, therefore, something the sick person has to offer the healthy. In the contract between doctor and patient, the dependent sick person's willingness to receive is part of the currency of the bargain.

The whole concept of the dependency of the sick helps focus our attention at this superficial, seemingly volitional level and away from the more threatening characteristics of the sick. The sick represent a threat to the rest of us by making us dangerously aware of the frailty of our own connectedness, the thinness of our shield of omnipotence, the incompetence of reason, and the transience of our control over our world. Segregating the sick in hospitals and providing them with special rules of behavior serve to mitigate the threat for both the sick person and the outside world, if not to eliminate it entirely.

As in so many other aspects of human behavior, we do not discuss or even secretly recognize the essential characteristics of sickness because it would be too frightening to do so. Ostensibly, the physician deals only with disease elements of the illness. His manifest function is the cure of disease, but his latent function, healing, which involves restoring the sick to the world of the healthy, is a secret even to himself.

2 Illness and Disease

GENERALLY SPEAKING, when someone in our society is ill he assumes that he has a disease, but how he feels is ill. When a great many people in two different cultures (New York City and rural Jamaica, West Indies) were asked what the phrase "being ill" meant to them, virtually all of them—little children, adults, the aged, and even physicians—responded by saying simply that it meant not being healthy. Being healthy was being fit, they said, being able to go or do when you want to. Being ill was being unfit or unable to do. No diseases were mentioned (except by very little children who talked about cuts and tummyaches and the like).

On the other hand, if you do feel ill and someone asks you what is the matter, you will commonly respond with the name of a disease. You will say, "I have sinusitis," instead of, "My head is clogged and I have a postnasal discharge." Or, rather than telling of the griping pains in your abdomen, you may say that your colitis is acting up. In other words, you will supply disease terms to explain the feelings of illness and assume that all such symptoms are caused by some disease or another, or that they are "emotional" in the sense of not being real.

However, the assumption that illness and disease are the same is, I believe, culturally derived. The assumption may be based on what has been repeatedly and objectively demonstrated, but it has also become a part of the beliefs of the culture of the so-called Western societies. As such, the assumption no longer depends for its existence on continued proof. It is now an article of faith against which other assumptions can be tested. It can be used as a basis for talking to your neighbor about your complaints, for teaching in medical schools, for delivering medical care, and even for providing kinds of health insurance. Since these last three activities seem to be in some trouble now, this might be a good time to examine the article of faith. Certainly, if disease and illness are not the same, curing and healing may well be very different functions; and what is good policy for one may not be good policy for the other.

I have suggested in the preceding chapter that there is a distinction between the disease of an organ of the body and the illness of the whole man, and indeed such a difference seems valid. We certainly base many of our complaints about doctors on just such a difference. We say, "All the doctor seems to care about are my kidneys; he doesn't care about me"—and we know what we mean, or think we do. From this point on, let us use the word "illness" to stand for what the patient feels when he goes to the doctor and "disease" for what he has on the way home from the doctor's office. Disease, then, is something an organ has; illness is something a man has.

Although the word "disease" literally means "removed from ease," we generally use it to mean a disturbance of the organs or body fluids characterized by structural alteration or biochemical change. We have come to speak and act as though without the evidence of such alteration or change there is no illness—nothing justifying medical attention: "If someone doesn't have a disease, he shouldn't be wasting a doctor's time." (When the American Medical Association gave alcoholism the status of a disease, it became all right to transfer its victims from jail to the doctor's office.)

The important thing to recognize is the definition of disease on which we act, on which the functions of both physician and patient, and their manifest interactions, are based.

It is certainly not so in every culture. In primitive cultures when people are ill (unfit, unable to do) and seek help, neither they nor those who will help have a similar conception of disease to ours. Nonetheless, some framework exists to "explain" the illness and on which to base a remedy. More important, though the practitioner may be deprived of the benefit of Western science, his remedy is often effective (among the people of any culture, no practitioner lasts long who does not return patients to health).

The Navaho Indians in Arizona have been exposed to Western medicine for about a hundred years and quite intensively in recent years. The Navahos have resisted Christianity; their own religion with its inherent concept of illness has remained a viable part of their culture. The function of the Navaho medicine man is to bring in good and drive out evil (and man is surrounded by dangers on all sides). As John Adair and Kurt Deuschle tell us in their report on public health among the Navahos, a healing ceremony is "a complex interweaving of praying, chanting, and painting, medication with herbal infusions and other procedures which are carried out by exactly prescribed means. . . . The Navahos believe that they are performing the songs and rituals that the gods used to bring about creation. It is more than re-enactment, it is the real thing, it is the laying of their hands on the machinery of the infinite and straightening it out."

In 1955 a Navaho medicine man who was also a tribal leader spoke at a monthly meeting of white physicians gathered at Fort Defiance. "There are some things which we medicine men know the white doctor is better able to cure than we, such as appendicitis and tuberculosis; we have given up on these. Then there are such things as snake bite, which both the medicine man and the doctor can cure, each using his own method. But there is still a third kind of illness which only the Navaho medicine man can cure—for example, a person might have lightning illness, caused by his being nearby when lightning struck. You white doctors wouldn't know that person is sick and so it wouldn't occur to you to treat that person. But, in the Navaho way of thinking, it is just as important to treat him as it is to treat the person in pain with appendicitis."

It is important to realize that this is the statement of a sophisticated man in a culture that has accepted Western medicine where it is useful.

In every culture unfitness is presented to healers in ways that depend on the beliefs of the particular culture. In our culture the only form of unfitness that can be acceptably presented to physicians is that which can be called disease. Yet I believe that we, too, have disabilities that are not specifically connected to disease (to alteration of body fluids or structures) and that in the past, in conformity with cultural convention, were hidden in the symptoms of disease and were treated by doctors as such.

The drama of medical care is carried out in the arena

of society; and while the primary roles are played by patient and doctor, other members of the social group also play active roles. In our culture the rules for this interplay seem to have been stable for a long time, but today the rules are changing because of the technological revolution of our times. In the last generation profound changes in disease patterns and the hope of cure for the first time ever in the world's history have forcibly separated illness and disease. The success of medicine has created a strain: the doctor sees his role as the curer of disease and "forgets" his role as a healer of the sick, and patients wander disabled but without a culturally acceptable mantle of disease with which to clothe the nakedness of their pain.

In all cultures people go to their doctors because they *feel* uncomfortable, unusual, or unpleasant; but it is a feeling—or something they think they feel. Even when you go to the doctor with pneumonia, it is not pneumonia that makes you go. You go because you feel sick and feverish and have a cough and perhaps chest pain or some other unpleasant feelings. The doctor "gives" you pneumonia to explain your feelings.

In the days when frontiersmen fought the American Indians, both occasionally contracted pneumonia and sometimes succumbed. It is one of the things that can happen to animals with lungs. The frontiersman had "pneumonia," which his doctor could define in anatomical and pathological terms. Certain objective causal relationships were established, and the whole provided a structure of reason from which the doctor could act and could answer the pioneer's inevitable questions. On the other hand, the Indian who had the same symptoms was invaded by spirits. His doctor and his culture had also established causal relationships and had even, perhaps, provided more satisfying answers to the question of why the Indian had his illness. It is very necessary to remember that in those days the white doctor's treatment really may have been no more effective than the medicine man's treatment! It is important to realize that our way of conceiving of disease, our rational scientific basis of medicine, is part of our Western cultural heritage and may not be the only "correct" picture or the only answer to the questions "what" or "why" posed by the sick person. "What is the matter with me?" and "Why did it happen?" are very personal, as well as general, questions.

With good cause, we have great confidence in the biochemical and cellular basis for disease revealed by our scientific method. But to understand it in the present context, to make the vital distinction between illness and disease, between healing and curing, it is necessary to abstract ourselves from this concept of disease sufficiently to realize that it is also a cultural development. In broad terms, there has been no time when we did not think that we knew where disease came from.

We have always had explanations, and we have always believed our explanations correct. Indeed, it is one of the miracles of optimistic mankind that again and again it has had such faith in the "facts" of today when, if there is one thing the history of science should have taught us, it is that our most dearly beloved scientific beliefs are fragile in the face of time.

As we briefly trace the development of scientific medicine, we shall see how the two functions of physicians, healing and curing, have become separated and how, at least in part, it is the overwhelming success of curing that has caused the breach.

Our system of explanations, our rational basis of medicine, like so much of the basis of our rational Western culture, we owe in large part to the Greeks. Hippocrates, who was born about 460 B.C., is called the father of modern medicine primarily because he introduced the use of observation as a basis for the diagnosis and therapy of disease and rejected a system of medicine that depended entirely on magico-religious beliefs. He introduced objectivity into medicine as part of a culture that was similarly using observation to lay down a basis for rational and systematic development in many areas of man's activity. Among his contemporaries were Socrates, Plato, Sophocles, and Aristophanes.

It is not necessary here to solve the philosophical problem of whether Hippocrates or his contemporaries, when they looked at a fractured ankle, were perceiving the same thing as physicians who see a fractured ankle today. Surely perception is influenced by the social context of the observer. However, one of the truly wonderful things about medicine is that it is rooted in the body, and to the body it must always return to test the validity of its beliefs.

It is little wonder that many of Hippocrates's observations are so valid today; a fractured ankle in 400 B.C. and a fractured ankle in A.D. 1976 look the same because the anatomy of the ankle is the same. While perception may indeed be influenced by the social context and the ankle may be differently clad in different cultures, the ankle remains the ankle. We may borrow, in this regard, Hippocrates's impatience with philosophers whose view of the body rested more on speculation than on observation. This brief evidence that philosophers were at odds with physicians even then is confirmed by an assertion in one of

Plato's dialogues that if a doctor and a cook were to discuss food, the cook would make the doctor look the fool (Hippocratic therapy was, in good part, dietetics). Nonetheless, Hippocrates's theory of medicine was based on the physical philosophy of his time, which believed in a spiritual essence diffused through the whole works of creation and striving to preserve things in their natural state and to restore them when they became deranged. "Nature," said Hippocrates, "is the physician of diseases." How congenial that sounds to us, though his theories of cause and of the elements and humors (fire, water, black bile, etc.) are totally foreign. During his long life Hippocrates described, classified, and suggested rational therapies for a large number of diseases with lasting accuracy. He also provided the image of the ideal physician that has persisted (at least in the minds of patients) to this day—calm and effective, humane and observant, prompt and cautious, at once learned and willing to learn, pure in mind and body, and fearing only lest he fail to serve. (While I use the name of Hippocrates as though I were writing of one man, it seems clear that the writings of Hippocrates are the work of many physicians of the same school of thought.)

Thus the age of Hippocrates was the age of medicine in which magic gave way to reason based on observation. But while we tend to remember the acuteness of his observation, we are apt to forget that throughout all the writings were recognition of and great respect for the therapeutic effects of the unknown healing forces of nature. The same forces in wider context were the concern of his contemporaries, as Aristotle's discussion of psyche (soul) so clearly and fully illustrates.

One of the ironies of the history of medicine dating to classical Greece that still profoundly affects us is that the Hippocratic school of medicine, sharing the rationalism of the Golden Age of Greece, no longer looked for the causes of disease in divine retribution, the invasion of demons, or the disturbance of evil spirits. Diseases, these physicians said, were natural things, arising from natural causes. The causes of disease could be found within the constitution of men and in disturbances in their inner and outer equilibriums resulting from diet or heredity or from a maladaptation to their inner or outer environments. For example, before their time epilepsy was considered to be a sacred disease, a visitation from the gods. And so the following opening passage of the book *On the Sacred Disease* from the works of Hippocrates was revolutionary.

It is thus with regard to the disease called Sacred: it appears to me to be no wise more divine nor more sacred than other diseases, but has a natural cause from which it originates like other affections. Man regards its nature and cause as divine from ignorance and wonder, because it is not at all like other diseases. And this notion of its divinity is kept up by their inability to comprehend it and the simplicity of the mode by which it is cured, for men are freed from it by purifications and incantations. But if it is reckoned divine because it is wonderful, instead of one there are many diseases which would be sacred; for, as I will show, there are others no less wonderful and prodigious, which nobody imagines to be sacred.

In such words lie the roots of Western scientific medicine. The irony comes from the fact that the same school of physicians, with their drive for rationalism and objectivity, were casting aside the use of the spoken word in medicine and were laying the basis for the modern physician who does not speak to his patients.

The origins of the lack of communication between doctor and patient, the Spanish medical historian Pedro Lain Entralgo shows us, come from two sources. The first was that the Hippocratic physicians were so eager to separate themselves from the superstitious and popular medicine they superseded that they disavowed the spoken or sung charms, chants, and incantations that were formerly the primary modes of treatment. The use of the word in treatment was suspect, since it smacked of those earlier superstitions. The second source of silence was the fact that the Hippocratic school based its diagnosis and treatment on objective measurement. While objective measurement included the information of the senses, it decidedly did not include much of what the patient said, since that was merely opinion. Thus Virgil called medicine "the silent art." And all this in the age when Aristotle was developing the importance of the word and when men were valued most highly for their ability to speak and convince through the use of the word, which was seen as the bridge between men. As medicine laid aside the word, it also laid aside part of the connection between the patient and his disease and the patient and his doctor.

In looking at the history of medicine, we are tracing the history of Western culture's attempt to answer the questions illness raises in the sick person: What is wrong with me? Why did it happen to me? What is going to happen because of this thing that has gone wrong?

There is both a narrow and a wide class of answers.

The narrow class of answers is specific to the problem. "What is wrong with me?" "You have a fractured ankle." To the wider question, "Why did I get epilepsy?" the answer prior to Hippocrates's time would have been, "It is the royal sickness." The wider class of questions has to do with fate and the relation of man to his universe. This latter formulation sounds mysterious precisely because of the direction the development of science and medicine has taken. Before Hippocrates, and probably for most of the other cultures of our present world, *only* the problem of fate, the wider question "Why *me?*" was pertinent, and the answers were provided by religion or mysticism.

When Hippocrates introduced the rational basis of medicine, he did not deny the cogency of the wider question. Rather, he introduced a systematic method of understanding and answering the narrower questions. What is the matter with the ankle? What should one do for the ankle? What will happen to the ankle?

In the period that followed classical Greece, the two classes of questions became muddled in the theological overgrowth. But with the birth of science during the Renaissance, the classes of questions split again. For society as a whole, God and Christianity gave weight to the soul and answered the seemingly mystical personal questions of illness.

For many of the scientists of the time such "simple" answers did not suffice, and in the seventeenth and eighteenth century a number of theories about the basic forces of life were advanced in an attempt to bring those forces within the realm of reason and to deny their mysticism. There was Descartes, who said that all life could be explained on a mechanical basis; there were other scientists who attempted to explain all animal activity on a chemical basis; and finally there were the vitalists, who believed in a mysterious life-force, a sensitive soul, a "phlogiston" whose effects were brought about by chemical process. To Descartes the body was a machine; to the vitalists it was the quintessence of nonmachine. While modern science has long surpassed the research contributions made by the theorists, their questions are still cogent and the basic arguments remain alive and active today—if not in science, then in the questing world.

It is interesting to speculate about Descartes's effect on medicine down through the ages since he formulated the mind-body duality. A cynic may see the Cartesian duality as a tremendously effective solution to the political problem that weighed down the development of science—the Church. By dividing man into mind and body as separate realities and by giving the body over to science and the mind (soul) to philosophy and religion, scientists were able to work without invading the province of God. Whatever the basis of the duality, it is more a part of our cultural unconscious than most of us ever realize. In any event, science emerged from the seventeenth century dedicated to a method of thought and having a mission to measure the finite. From that thought mode and mission it has not since deviated. Furthermore, it was in that same historical period that science laid its hand on medicine with a subsequently ever-tightening and jealous grip.

Pursuing the narrower questions of cause has served medicine well.

To understand the history of modern medicine (since the eighteenth century), one must visualize the world of disease in the 1700s. Disease and death were the commonplace of life. To say merely that life expectancy was short would be to miss the meaning of shortened life. In the eighteenth century infant mortality was devastating, and infection and its foster parent, malnutrition, underlaid the carnage. But infection did not stop in infancy. The diseases we dismiss lightly today, the ordinary contagious diseases of childhood, were then commonly fatal. Young adults died of pneumonia, streptococcal infections, and the non-specific diarrheal diseases. Epidemics were common (the Great Plague of 1665 killed more than 68,000 people in London), and bubonic plague and smallpox, far from confining themselves to sweeping through the land in fatal waves, remained in constant threatening residence. By the time they reached adulthood, the large majority of the population had already had smallpox. (At one time in Europe, almost everybody who was anybody had syphilis.)

The threat of these infectious diseases, as we all know so well by now, is greatly increased by crowding and improper hygiene. The industrial revolution with its rush to the cities helped foster disease in the rising populations. Sewage ran in the city streets. The slums were crowded beyond belief; there were no toilets and no running water, and lice and hunger and filth were everywhere. Modern travelers to India are shocked by similar scenes that nonetheless represent a distinct improvement over London or Paris in the eighteenth and early nineteenth centuries. The gap between rich and poor was huge, but the plague-bearing flea jumped it lightly.

Contagion was not the only threat. The diseases with which we are familiar were also prevalent. Minor trauma held the danger of blood poisoning, and simple fractures led to permanent disability. Cancer, appendicitis, and ulcers all occurred and commonly doomed sufferers to early death because surgery lay weighted down by unbearable pain and mortal infection.

Throughout this period mankind looked to God for surcease from disease and death. In earlier times the flagellants protected themselves from plague by incredible self-punishment. The source of disease, they said, lies within each man; the good will escape.

In retrospect, it seems that the people did well to look to God because doctors were not of much use. The treatment of individual cases was a horror. The tools available to physicians were rarely effective, and treatment consisted largely of bleeding, purgatives, and emetics. Fads in therapeutics rose and faded, based on the authority of their innovators rather than on acceptable evidence of usefulness. And yet, then as in ancient times, physicians made some patients better—but how?

In the late 1600s Thomas Sydenham, an English physician, began to bring order into the art of medicine. Following the Hippocratic tradition, he rediscovered the importance of knowing the natural history of disease; he also appreciated and wrote of the healing force of nature. He began to separate the fevers and gave accurate and beautiful descriptions of disease. His lead was followed by others, and by the beginning of the nineteenth century diseases were well catalogued and delineated. The step was essential to the development of treatment and the systematic teaching of medicine. Disease was cataloged in terms of the organs afflicted, the types of fevers, the presence of tumors—in other words, in terms of the patient's symptoms and the doctor's findings in his physical examination; the description was individual and largely subjective. Illness and disease were the same because disease was defined in terms of the types of unfitness.

By the mid-nineteenth century mankind was already being lifted out of the morass of disease—not by cure, because there was none, but by preventive medicine. The first advance was vaccination, but much more important was the great sanitary revolution that started in England in the 1830s; it was initiated by laymen, and physicians played little part until it was well along. The sanitary revolution is responsible not only for modern water supplies and sewage, government departments of health and sanitary laws, but for our entire attitude toward cleanliness and health. That attitude, now deeply ingrained in our culture, wards off disease with greater force than does chlorine in the water or any law.

The germ theory of disease that was developed and gained acceptance largely through the work of Louis Pasteur, Joseph Lister, and Robert Koch in the late 1800s began to give scientific answers to questions of disease causality. It had been known for a long time that there was an infectious principle—some matter by which certain diseases were transmitted. But muddled in with this concept were all sorts of vagaries including moral judgments that related the acquiring of a disease to the sufferer's intemperance or turpitude. To scientists that deplorable inexactitude ended with the discovery of bacteria as a cause of disease. Born was a clean exactness—one cause, one disease—which is now only beginning to be superseded by our increasing awareness of multiple causes.

Somewhat earlier than the development of the germ theory of disease, a German pathologist named Rudolf Virchow laid down the cellular basis of disease. In essence, the theory states that in all diseases there are structural changes at the cellular level and those changes are specific for each disease.

The germ theory and the cellular basis of disease together determined our present definition of disease. Diseases are entities in which there is structural change and for which unique cause can be found. The further history of medicine, for all its incredible advance, has changed the definition only by adding to it biochemical change (and underlying genetic defects); disease may have structural and/or biochemical change.

From the mid-nineteenth century until the 1930s, medicine progressed by fulfilling the potential of the germ theory and Virchow's pathology.

The age of cure might be dated from the advent of the sulfonamides in the 1930s. From that time forward the rate of development of effective therapy has increased exponentially. The individual effectiveness of the modern physician against diseases can be described only in superlatives. Not only in treatment but also in diagnosis, technological progress has made the neophyte physician of today far superior to the experienced specialist of a generation ago.

The tools are magnificent; the drugs are fantastically effective; the electronic technology is a wonder to behold. And yet it is in the midst of this justified hyperbole that we find it necessary to see what has gone wrong. So let us look again at the structure of the history of medicine.

In discussing the evolution of our present concepts of disease, I write as though disease were a "thing," an "it." Certainly common usage supports that way of speaking. We say that someone got pneumonia, tuberculosis, or cancer, but we mean equally that cancer or tuberculosis got the person. We even speak of a heart attack as though it were a thing, despite the fact that we really know that a heart attack is only an incident occurring in the course of the disease called arteriosclerosis.

The way in which we now speak of diseases as things, as independent entities, represents the outcome of a long struggle that took place from 400 B.C. to the nineteenth century. This dispute was between what are called the physiologists (Hippocrates, for example) and the ontologists. The ancient physiologists held that disease was an imbalance of the "humors" of a patient and came about primarily from an abnormal relationship of man and his environment. In more modern terms, it would be said that the cause and the nature of disease are determined by the nature of the sick individual and can be understood only in the context of the individual's environment. (See how congenial that sounds to us today.) In contrast, the ontologists believed that diseases had their own being, that they were entities or things that invaded the sick person. You can readily see that the germ theory of disease was the victorious weapon of the ontologists, which sounded the death knell for the view of the physiologists. Even though Virchow knew the danger of confusing the cause of a disease (for example, the germ of tuberculosis) with the disease itself (tuberculosis), he was a complete ontologist. To him diseases were things that could be seen in the microscope. (It is one of the ironies of medical history that the work of Rudolf Virchow, who himself was an ardent humanist and balanced thinker, drove humanism—a primary concern for the sick person—underground with such force that we are just now beginning to recover the balance.)

The key difference between the physiologists and the ontologists was the importance of the sick individual. It may now be clear why the individual seems secondary in importance to disease in present-day medicine with its ontological heritage.

There have been three lines of growth: the search for exact definitions of disease, the search for causes, and the search for cure. The route these searches have taken is the bequest of science and the ontological viewpoint to medicine. Our science is based on the measurement of the finite, the rendering of the phenomena into numbers. It is common to confuse the question we are asking with the method we use to get the answer. Yet the method used determines the nature of the answer. If we were asked to describe a rose and we were given only a ruler to do it, the picture of the rose that emerged would be solely in terms of inches. The picture would be true but incomplete. If a ruler were our only way of describing things, we would not know that the picture was incomplete. Our knowledge of the universe is a function of our technology, and technology is a function of our philosophical view of the universe.

The three searches that pervade the history of medicine—*what, why, what can we do about it*—are universal. But illness is a special phenomenon. It has both objective and personal aspects, and thus the questions have both an objective and a personal meaning. The search for definitions of illness was essential to provide a basis for any further inquiry, but it is clear to anybody who has ever been ill that the ontological definitions of disease that have emerged from our history in terms of structural and chemical change and that leave out the individual are an incomplete picture of illness. The complete picture would involve other, more personal phenomena.

Similarly, the question "why" asked by the person who is ill is of much greater dimension than the question "why" asked by the medical researcher. The person is really asking: "Why me? What did I do that causes me to get sick?"—to which wider questions the germ theory of disease offers only narrow answers, vitally important but incomplete.

Since the development of cure is dependent on knowing the *what* and the *why* of disease, it is clear that cure will be directed only against those objective manifestations of illness that our science has defined as disease. Thus curing the disease will be effective in resolving the illness in proportion to the degree that the illness is explained by the disease. Where all the symptoms and disordered feelings that make up illness are explained by the disease, as in streptococcal sore throat, the cure of the sore throat will resolve the illness. But in tuberculosis, where the disordered feelings, disconnectedness from the society, and numerous other ramifications of the disease are widespread and pervasive, curing—killing the tubercle bacillus—represents only part of returning the patient to health—a vital part perhaps, but only a part.

The following examples may make the relationship between disease and illness clearer.

Through most of our adult lives most of us have a disease called arteriosclerosis. We are, for the large majority of that time, not ill from it. Similarly, hypertension and diabetes exist through the majority of their natural history without associated illness. Even cancer, as we all know, can be present for long periods without symptoms.

On the other hand, it is possible to have illness without disease. While hypochondriasis may leap to mind, it probably represents a less common example. We are talking about not feeling well, about having symptoms. In those terms all of us have been ill without having disease. Sometimes we went to doctors and were reassured that we had no disease. More often, we went and were given diagnoses such as low blood pressure, tilted uterus, or hypoglycemia with which to keep our symptoms honorable (although such diagnoses do not represent disease). And often we just felt ill for a few days, and our discomfort passed without our visiting the doctor. The continuing need for diagnoses such as hypoglycemia is made clear by the persistence of that diagnosis. Into and out of popularity it passes. No matter that objective evidence rarely supports it; back it comes with the regularity of locusts. Its current vogue can be attributed to articles in the lay press, primarily in women's magazines, that tell us, "Doctors do not understand how common the problem is because they have not been trained to discover the diagnosis." It is certainly true that doctors do not give legitimacy to the diagnosis as a disease (except rarely) because it does not fit our exacting criteria. But in the demand for this diagnosis, we see how important it is that illnesses be given a legitimate name, that a sufferer have a mantle for his distress that society will accept.

I remember a young woman who had been sent home from her first term in college because she had hypoglycemia. Her parents brought her to me along with the laboratory report that was supposed to prove the diagnosis. I found the results inconclusive and repeated the many-hours-long test in my office. While this was going on, I talked to her and examined her. She was indeed symptomatic: her appetite was poor; she had difficulty sleeping and concentrating; she had headaches and cried frequently.

Making the diagnosis of homesickness and depression in this girl from a close family who was away from home for the first time required little sophistication and took less time than doing the test (which was normal, but which had to be done anyway).

There can, of course, be coexistent illness and disease. For much of the world's history and for much of the present world population, that is probably the most common form. Even here, however, things are not so simple. The huge incidence of infant and child wastage in the underdeveloped countries comes largely from the diarrhea-pneumonia symptom complex (64 percent of all deaths in the age group 1 to 4 in Egypt). Despite repeated attempts, it has been impossible to demonstrate that one bacterium or virus is responsible; the symptom complex seems to result from a mixture of problems of hygiene and nutrition. It is not caused by a "named" disease but rather represents a classical example of the interaction of culture and biology leading to death.

Even when illness and disease coexist, it is possible to demonstrate their distinction from each other. An elderly man, after losing his wife, continued to work at his job in a department store, but his clothing and personal habits became sloppy and his appetite was poor. He caught a cold that persisted, with a cough that grew increasingly worse. After about two weeks he developed a fever; he was found to have pneumonia and admitted to the hospital. Despite apparently adequate therapy and an initially good response, his fever persisted and he lay listless in the bed, saying that he didn't care what happened and would as soon be dead. His doctor delivered a scathing lecture to him based on the patient's lifelong religious and moral beliefs, and the next day the old man was obviously better. On the day after that, free of fever and almost free of his cough, he signed himself out of the hospital. However, he was furious (perhaps rightly so) at the doctor for not allowing him to give in to his illness.

The distinction between illness and disease has been buried, first by the overwhelming prevalence of disease that has been our heritage and second by the rise of scientific medicine, whose methodology and philosophy have tended to deny the existence of that which it cannot measure and to disclaim the importance of the individual in relation to his sickness.

The rise of psychiatry in the twentieth century established that there is validity in what we cannot measure. Certainly, the growth of psychiatry during this century and the contributions of Freud must be counted as a major medical advance. Freud showed us for the first time in a systematic way the presence of the unconscious mind and many of its operations. He made clear, in an undeniable manner, the influence of early childhood experience on subsequent behavior. He introduced a mode of therapy comparable to no previous way of making people better.

Many of the facts of unconscious behavior are apparent to any person with open eyes, an open mind, and children. Our world has changed because of these revelations, and we shall never go back. No people at any time in the world's history have ever had such self-awareness. Yet we argue about many of these concepts as though they hadn't been around for more than fifty years and the illnesses described by them hadn't been known since the beginning of time! They do not fit any concept of disease that has evolved since Hippocrates, although the influence of emotions on bodily change had been appreciated even before Hippocrates. Indeed, we even find Freud banished from popularity in some circles.

These concepts cannot be quantified; there is no structure to examine under a microscope and, with few exceptions, no chemical to find altered in a blood test (not for lack of trying to find these changes, I assure you). They do not, in short, fit a philosophy of disease that took a long time to evolve. There are other reasons why they are difficult for doctors to accept (doctors being persons and these being very personal phenomena), but at least in part the profession's difficulty with these concepts stems from the fact that they are so "soft," so difficult to measure.

Increasingly in recent years some analytic psychiatrists have attempted to give their domain "hard" structure and bring it into line with the rest of medicine. In so doing, I believe that they have slowed progress in what should have been one of medicine's most exciting areas and that they have decreased the utility of these concepts for all of us.

The technical revolution in diagnosis is also upsetting the previous balance between illness and disease. More and more we are presented with disease not associated with illness; indeed, that is the thrust of preventive medicine. The yearly checkup is meant to reveal disease before it has a chance to produce illness. On the other hand, the so-called multiphasic health-screening programs, which are semi-automated checkups, have produced many findings (such as high uric acid in the blood or even slightly elevated blood sugar) usually associated with disease; but because they are found so "early," physicians are often in doubt about their significance. They do not know whether to tell the patient about the findings or what to tell him to do about them if he does know. Despite such problems, the multiphasic health-screening techniques, now experimental or at least in their youth, are going to be a major presence before long, prepackaged and sold by industry in volume.

Finally, technical advance has upset the balance between illness and disease (and healing and curing) because of the drastic changes in the disease patterns that it has wrought. For most of us in the Western world, premature death is no longer imminent. The death of infants is unusual, the death of children rare, and the death of young adults so improbable that it must be removed from the realistic possibilities of young life. The change is most clearly to be seen in women. Unwanted pregnancies and life-endangering abortion have been, or are, disappearing as threats to life. The necessity for many pregnancies to ensure a few surviving children has been eliminated by the decline in infant and child mortality. Disability resulting from gynecological disease has gone the way of the infectious diseases: increasingly rare, avoidable, or easily treatable. For the aged also, the pattern has changed; thus we commonly see persons in their seventies who are healthy and functional and no longer "old" by the standards of our world.

The fact that these changes in disease patterns have occurred coincidentally with the rise of technological medicine has enhanced the belief that technological medicine was responsible for the changes. There may be, as Dr. Warren Winkelstein has pointed out, good reason to dispute "the underlying belief among both the lay public and people in the technical professions that the quantity and quality of medical services are directly related to the health status of the population." This contention is perhaps best illustrated by the failure of experiments in which the resources of modern technological medicine have been brought to bear against the disease-ridden poor of some "backward" indigenous group in this country or elsewhere. These studies indicate that modern medicine is unable to alter significantly the basic pattern or prevalence of disease that existed prior to the experiments. Although the failures are often attributed to the unwillingness of the group under study to accept Western medicine or its tenets, at least one excellent investigation—the Navaho-Cornell Field Health Research Project, conducted from 1955 to 1960 and extremely well received by the Navaho Indians—makes it clear that such an explanation is too simple. Working in close cooperation with the tribal leaders, the study group brought modern medical services to the Navaho Indian reservation, providing a well-equipped ambulatory care facility, physicians, nurses, and trained Navaho health aides, and transportation for hospital care. All of this was introduced into an extremely poor environment, among non-literate people in extended families living in windowless, one-room log-and-mud dwellings with dirt floors.

Both the Navahos and the study group were pleased with the day-to-day achievements of the medical services in the reservation. By objective criteria the project had some successes to report: tuberculosis, a common problem among the Navahos, was sharply reduced, and so was the incidence of significant ear infections among children. But the really startling findings were on the negative side. Except for the above decreases, at the end of five years there was virtually no change in the overall disease pattern and little, if any, change in the death rates, including a shockingly high infant mortality rate that persisted at three times the national average. The investigators concluded that the disease and mortality patterns of the Navahos were a result of the way they lived and could not be changed until basic changes took place in the tribe's way of life.

Apparently medical care alone, no matter how well delivered or technically complete, cannot be expected to lift the burden of sickness. This point is further illustrated by the trends in the patterns of disease over the past two generations in America. Since the common infectious scourges of the past have disappeared more or less simultaneously with the growth and development of modern medicine and its technical wizardry, it is commonly believed that the dramatic improvement in the health of our society was brought about by the achievements of physicians and medical science. By and large, however, this is not true.

At the beginning of the twentieth century the pattern of disease in the United States and other Western nations showed a high overall death rate (about 28 deaths per 1,000 population per year, as against the present rate of about 9 per 1,000 per year) with a certain monotony of cause: pneumonia and influenza, tuberculosis, typhoid fever, and the various dysenteries. This high rate of mortality, as well as the specific pattern of diseases, was in part traceable directly to the urban social conditions brought on by the industrial revolution. Mass shifts of the rural population into the cities had resulted in poverty, crowding, and poor sanitation, providing fertile ground for the transmission of disease. In the United States the problem was compounded by the continuous influx of poverty-stricken immigrants.

In 1900 the annual death rate from tuberculosis in

the United States was 200 per 100,000. Throughout the next five decades the death rate fell rapidly and steadily, so that by the 1950s, when the first effective antituberculosis drugs became available, the annual rate was already below 20 per 100,000. Prior to the advent of the new drugs, whatever treatment was available was frequently ineffective and was restricted primarily to those who could afford it. It seems reasonable to speculate, then, in the absence of any clear evidence to the contrary, that the improvement in the mortality rates that took place before the 1950s resulted in large part from improved living conditions, including better nutrition and diminished crowding. (It is also true of an infectious disease such as tuberculosis that its decreasing incidence promotes a further diminution in the disease, simply because the fewer individuals carrying it, the lower are the chances of contracting the disease through contact.)

As with tuberculosis, so with typhoid. After 1905, cases of typhoid fever became steadily less common in American cities, so that by the time effective drugs became available typhoid was already a very rare disease. In years past it was usual to attribute the decrease to typhoid immunization, but we know now that the vaccine at best is not very effective; rather, the improvement can be traced to the introduction of good sanitation, to chlorination of the water supply, and to improvements in personal hygiene.

Perhaps the most gratifying change of all was the decrease in infant mortality during the early decades of this century in the United States. By far the greater part of this decrease can be attributed to the sharp reduction in the diarrhea-pneumonia complex that, as Dr. Walsh McDermott has noted, "occurred before there were any antimicrobial drugs at all; neither were there any vaccines for this disease complex. . . . The fall occurred during a time in which biomedical science and technology could put no specific, no decisive therapies or preventatives into the hands of our clinical physicians." Here again, no single reason for the improvement can be pointed out, but it can be noted that it occurred during a period in which standards of living, education, nutrition, and sanitation all improved.

In like manner, we are protected today against many food-borne diseases more by the life-style of our society than by anything specific we do for our health. It is the economics of modern food distribution, not considerations of health, that demands that foods be packaged and protected against spoilage or contamination. The rapid bankruptcy of a soup company after the press reports of a few cases of botulism caused by eating its canned soup illustrated dramatically how much more effectively health may be protected by the mass media than by food inspectors.

Our present pattern of death and disease, of course, is not merely what is left over after we have escaped the ravages of infectious diseases. Along with affluence and the good life for many of us has come a new pattern of disease: cancer, heart disease, stroke. Yet, just as medical care played a minor role in reducing death rates in the past, so we should not expect that it alone will relieve us of our present burdens. In fact, after fifty years of consistent decline in the mortality rates, we witnessed in the 1960s a new upward trend, particularly among white males. The connection of a single personal habit—cigarette smoking— with one disease, lung cancer, seems to have been proved. In the case of our worst epidemic, coronary heart disease, however, the chain of causation is more complex. Diet, level of activity, cigarette smoking, stress, as well as other factors, are so interrelated here that it is fair to say that a whole style of life is involved—the life-style characteristic of an affluent society. It would be naive to expect that medical science by itself can "cure" us of this condition. Even if present surgical techniques were perfected, the value of a new or repaired heart in the body of a patient whose life-style remained otherwise unchanged would not be very high.

The general health of populations, then, is not directly dependent on medical services. Medical care did not get us out of our past troubles, and it will not get us out of our present ones. These propositions should be self-evident, yet widespread confusion still remains on the subject. And the confusion continues to foster the belief among both laymen and physicians that doctors treat disease and that it is by treating disease that individuals and whole societies are made better. *Doctors do not treat disease; they treat patients who have diseases.* That distinction is obvious, so obvious that we often give it lip service without inquiring what the difference is between treating a disease and treating a patient with a disease. A patient is a person with both an illness and a disease; the patient is made better to the extent that both the illness and the disease are made better.

There is yet another reason why we have to dig and probe to separate illness and disease. That reason lies in the origin of those aspects of the sick that were discussed in Chapter 1.

The nondisease elements of the sick person that we have identified arise with the course of disease in the patient, but they are also separate from it. Just as dependency that occurs in sickness is also an independent entity that may persist past recovery from the disease, so, too, may these other elements remain when the biochemical or structural alterations that constitute the disease have returned to normal. The separateness of the elements of sickness can be clearly seen by the fact that in disease we do not have to be physically reconstituted to be well again. The amputee, minus his limb but again able to function, is again well.

There are several possible combinations: disconnectedness, loss of the sense of omnipotence and omniscience, and loss of control, in greater or lesser degree, may arise in illness caused by disease. These factors may arise from other causes and themselves be the cause of illness and perhaps of disease. We have seen how sickness brings forth these other elements; now let us see how they may promote illness.

The object is not to see how the factors that we have identified combine with the pneumococcus to cause pneumonia, although that is an intriguing thought, but how they present themselves in a culture whose system of illness is epitomized by pneumonia. The factors themselves, arising as they do from the structure of man much like the gallbladder, are presumed to be culture free, a universal attribute of the human organism. But when they are sufficiently intense to cause pain and thus to cause someone to search for help, they must be presented according to a system of illness congenial to the culture in order for the cry for help to be correctly identified and some therapy offered that will provide relief.

Loss of connectedness is as universal as loss itself. It is obvious that it is not only physical modalities such as the senses that bind us to the world but our emotional connections as well. These latter, though more difficult to define, play an even greater part in preventing us from "falling off the world." Our place in society, group identity, and our loved ones allow us to define ourselves. Without them we are nothing. What is important to recognize is that our very existence is defined by our relationships—our connection to life itself.

That this is true in more than a figurative sense seems clear from the lethal effect of forced separation, as noted earlier in reference to voodoo death. While that example is extreme, all of us have experienced, in one situation or another, the sharp distress caused by forced loss of connectedness. Few things provoke such intense pain. The pain of loss is described as physical: a constriction in the lower chest and upper abdomen; a feeling as though there were a very heavy weight in the abdomen. When we think of the distress of loss, however, we think of it in emotional terms: sorrow, depression, anxiety, fear, anger. But coincident are disabilities that are physically expressed: the pains noted before, loss of appetite, inattention, inability to work effectively, changes in pulse and blood pressure, and so on. We assume these to be the result of the emotional distress— a visceral expression of emotion. But for the moment and for understanding the function of healers, we are better served to see them as occurring alongside the verbalized emotional response. We are accustomed to examining these responses verbally (if only to ourselves)—that is, with language. We use the word "sad" to identify for ourselves and others the emotions and their physical counterparts. "How do you feel?" "My face is heavy-browed and stiff, my shoulders are tensed, my chest contracted and my stomach tight, my limbs heavy and clumsy." We don't say that; we say, "I am very sad."

With such words we inform others but, at the same time, reassure ourselves. We are reassured because, by identifying the sensation with the emotion, we contain the symptoms within the frame of rationality provided by language. But although associated, the physical feelings and the verbally expressed emotion are separate. One person may have all the physical sensations but may not verbalize the emotion. Others may verbalize the emotion, but we suspect that they feel none of the sensations. Thus far we are on familiar ground; that is, most of us recognize both the emotion and the associated sensations.

But let us picture the beginning of all this, the infant. Though it is unable at first to distinguish between itself and its world, nonetheless many things are happening. The happenings provoke sensory responses (sensations) that are both pleasant and unpleasant, and learning is going on all the while. At this period the entire learning experience is sensorimotor. Just as the infant cannot distinguish self from nonself, it seems safe to assume that it is unable to distinguish inner self from outer self; that is, sensations arising from its bladder and bowels, for example, may not be distinguished from sensations arising from its surrounding (ears and eyes) or its mother (touch or feeling tone).

As growth occurs and the infant begins to make distinctions between inner and outer self and between self and objects, previous learning is not obliterated. Repeated observations support the conclusion that early learning is qualitatively different—stronger and more persistent. Thus, until the time of speech, communication with the world is nonverbal, and the infant is not just a passive receptor; every parent knows with what force the "helpless" animal can use its own clumsy physicality to control its world.

Well before speech the physical definitions of comfort, security, love, fear, loss, inadequate control, sense of omnipotence, and so on are laid down; therefore, well before speech the individual has become acculturated in what are acceptable modes of physical expression.

We learn from Piaget that when speech comes along, the child does not merely take his old experience and apply words to it; rather, he regresses somewhat and relearns much behavior, now in the symbolic terms of language. The old set of physical relationships with the world (and with the inner self) fades into the past, but I do not believe that it disappears. We act from there on as though things for which we do not have words do not exist. The kind of intelligence that appears with language, as Piaget shows us, supplants the previous sensory intelligence or rational physicality—the ability to do or react with the environment in a repetitively effective way.

It must be remembered that the kind of thinking represented by language is not the only way to relate to the world; it is just more effective. Language or thought allows for a kind of experimental symbolic action interposed between the impulse and real action.

With increasing language comes increasing acculturation and thus knowledge of the ways in which distress will be accepted by one's particular world. It is now easier to see why we use the word "sad" to stand for the array of physical feelings that may accompany loss or disconnectedness. It should also be easier to see why there may be many disordered sensations connected with loss that are not identified with the symbolic word in our awareness, since they may represent culturally unacceptable responses.

Disconnectedness, of which loss is just one example,

can, then, be associated with many physical feelings that are not present in the healthy, "fit" person. We can call these physical feelings "symptoms" and understand that they may be presented to a doctor as such, but it is highly unlikely that they would be presented to the doctor as "disconnectedness." The origin of the symptoms is buried deeply in the development of the patient, inaccessible to his awareness and equally inaccessible to the awareness of his physician.

Failure of the sense of indestructibility is another problem of the sick person. But a feeling of omnipotence is necessary to daily functioning. It is equally assaulted by automobile accidents and business failures. It helps keep our brave face toward the hostile world. It, too, plays a part in the development of symptoms, since the person with a shattered sense of omnipotence is ill—not fit. A shattered sense of omnipotence is not a suitable diagnosis for our medical marketplace. In the same way the inability to control our world may be a cause of unfitness, just as it may result from disease, but it, too, will not be acceptable in the medical market.

Such lack of fitness must be presented in terms acceptable to the patient, the doctor, and the society around them. Symptoms of disease are acceptable in our culture. In years past, legions of patients carried labels such as low blood pressure, low blood sugar, anemia, weak heart, heart murmur, arthritis, high blood pressure, and underactive thyroid to explain their symptoms and offer a basis for treatment. Now we know why the diagnosis of low blood sugar keeps coming back into vogue.

In recent years the symptoms of emotional disturbance have become acceptable terms for presenting unfitness in much of our society. The patient is allowed to be nervous, depressed, "emotional," and so forth, and he will still be well received. In New York, at least, these terms have become so acceptable to laymen and even to some doctors that they threaten to depose bodily disease. Fifteen years ago it was necessary for the doctor to be quite delicate in implying that someone's basic problem might be emotional; now, even with blood gushing from a wound, it is difficult to convince many that it is not emotional.

It is vital to remember that just as some "organic" disease may be merely a culturally acceptable package in which to hide causes of illness of which the patient is unaware, so, too, "emotional" disease can become an acceptable loss of fitness. When this occurs, the patient does not present the physician and the world with a problem truly related to his unfitness but rather adapts his real unfitness to predefined problems acceptable to the group. "When this happens," says Lévi-Strauss, "the value of the system [in his discussion, psychoanalysis] *will no longer* be based upon real cures from which certain individuals can benefit, but on the sense of security that the group receives from the myth underlying the cure and from the popular system upon which the group's universe is reconstructed." (My italics.) The concept of emotional disease becomes part of the body of cultural myths, as do cures and therapies based on it. It does not matter whether the source of the illness or the cure is "true"; accepting it as the source is an act of faith.

For the most rational among us, purely abstract reasoning about bacterial diseases and their cures is virtually impossible; we simply do not have enough information. A case in point is the ease with which viruses have been accepted as the cause of virtually everything not otherwise explained. Illness, as we have seen, disturbs the individual's own intactness, since it threatens his connectedness to his group and world. Illness in an individual also threatens the group, since it exposes them to the possibility of the same threat to themselves. It does not matter whether the source of the disruption is "real" (as in bacterial pneumonia) or otherwise, since neither the individual nor the group really understands the "real" (the causative bacteria), any more than having an awareness of the other hidden sources of illness. The group accepts the germ theory of disease and as such, to paraphrase the quote from Lévi-Strauss, "the value of the system [now real bacterial and viral etiology of disease] is no longer based upon real cures from which certain individuals can benefit, but on the sense of security that the group receives from the myth underlying the cure and from the popular system upon which the group's universe is reconstructed."

The fit person is at home in his world, connected to the people around him and in control of his body, his actions, and his world without necessarily being aware of any of these things. The sick person qualitatively differs in all these respects, although obviously to a varying degree. These differences may arise from disease or from another source; but whatever the source, help is needed to draw the person back into the group. The exact nature of the help needed is unknown to the sufferer, since the real nature of the disturbance is below awareness or beyond reason.

Rational thought processes, at least as they are communicated, are useful only in handling material that is known and that can be converted into language. Analytic reason operates on symbols. But the nature and source of the disturbances that we have seen to be present in illness are beyond the limited confines of language for several reasons: because some of the factors involved arose during a period of individual development that occurred prior to language; because the disturbances involve defenses, such as the sense of omnipotence and denial, that are essential to life but that would be inoperable if they were known in all their dimensions; because repression and denial push facets of the illness beyond the grasp of volition; but most of all because the ultimate cause is beyond reason, since it involves fate. Beyond reason lies magic, and thus much of illness lies in the realm of magic.

The history of Western medicine has followed lines of development started by Hippocrates as he replaced divine faith by painstaking observation. The succeeding centuries have brought many of the disease processes into the reach of reason but have decreased the importance of the individual in the scheme of disease. Despite the great understanding of the present day and the marvelous potential for cure, patients seem curiously unsatisfied with their physicians. Perhaps one explanation of the dissatisfaction is now clear. Each answer of medical science has explained a manifestation of disease; but the answer, and even the cure based on it, may fail to pull the patient back into the world. Each answer has pushed the border of the unknown further back but has failed to banish it. But more, the answers are for disease, and disease is but one part of illness. Science does not serve patients in some unembodied manner; it does so through their doctors—in the relationship between patient and doctor.

3 Doctor and Patient

On a monday in January I was asked to care for an eighty-six-year-old man who had been admitted to the hospital because of a stroke. His right side was paralyzed and he was unable to speak, difficulties that did not improve in the first week of hospitalization. The family said that his health had been deteriorating for the six months prior to admission. Though he had previously been a vigorous person, his memory and the workings of his mind had progressively declined so that before the stroke he was a failed old man. Considering the progressive nature of his illness, a neurologist who saw the patient in consultation suggested the possibility of a brain tumor. The neurologist wanted to do an angiogram (an X ray of the blood vessels of the brain) and had scheduled the test for the following Tuesday. When he discussed this with the family, however, they indicated that no matter what the X rays revealed, they would not consent to surgery.

By Friday evening the patient had developed a temperature of 103 degrees Fahrenheit and had become comatose. I was not called and did not learn of this development until I made my rounds the next day and read the events on the chart. The intern had diagnosed pneumonia and ordered blood cultures, nose, throat, and sputum cultures, and a urine culture from the indwelling catheter. Intravenous fluids with an appropriate dose of ampicillin (a kind of penicillin) were being administered.

I was distressed that antibiotic therapy had been started, since pneumonia could be a short, painless way of enabling this old man to escape the "cold degradations of decay." I wanted to write orders discontinuing his antibiotics but found myself hesitating to do so—a hesitancy at odds with my belief that there is a time to die for everyone and that the time had come for this old man, giving me no right to interfere. But then I saw from the front of the chart that he was allergic to penicillin (a fact the intern had apparently overlooked), and with relief at the excuse I wrote the order stopping the ampicillin.

Clinical experience is in conflict with the intern's actions. The overwhelming probability was that this eighty-six-year-old man would soon die no matter what was done. But there *are* miracles. Such patients do sometimes recover and live for months institutionalized, with accumulating problems of incontinence and bedsores, infection, and neglect—a slowly eroding death few among us would choose for ourselves or our parents. Nevertheless, did I have the right to decide to let this man die?

This not unusual case illustrates the dilemma that increasingly confronts doctors. While the public complains increasingly that physicians seem more concerned with disease and science than with their patients, each exciting technological advance has given physicians a greater power over life and death than ever before. With each advance has come profound ethical questions. A capability for organ transplantation raises the issue of scarce resources and the decision as to which patient will receive the new kidney or lung or liver that will allow him to live. Resuscitative power forces decisions about when to turn the respirator off, how to define death, and, indeed, whether or not a particular patient should be resuscitated in the first place. Who will make these decisions? Will it be doctors? Will it be a committee? a judge? a clergyman?

We are all familiar with the problem and with the criticism of physicians that suggests as part of the problem the very fact that they do make decisions about such matters. Indeed, some critics have asserted that physicians should not have the right to make any moral decisions. They do not argue that no man should have such power over another's life, because they are aware that in the real world decisions *must* be made; rather, they declare that *doctors* should not make such decisions. (One attorney with whom I have worked on ethical questions in medicine told me how shocked he was when he first discovered the scope of the physicians' responsibility; he said, "I was always taught that only the law had the power to take a man's life.")

The concern of these critics may be voiced in two ways. The first suggests that doctors have no inherent right to make decisions in the larger ethical issues for which they have no expertise. The second implies that physicians, by the very nature of their work, have a diminished moral awareness, caring more for their science or for disease than for their patients; blinded by "value-free" science, they are insensitive to the moral problems raised by their work. These criticisms seem supported by the frequent denial of physicians that they ever make moral decisions; they claim instead to make only technical decisions.

It seems clear, however, from the history of medicine and from the daily realities of medical practice that much of what physicians do concerns human values. A physician practicing his profession in the care of the sick is not operating in a cultural vacuum. His patient is not a collection of static facts wrapped in human form.

I believe that medicine is inherently a moral profession—or a moral-technical profession, if you wish. The practice of medicine—caring for the sick—takes what are presumed to be facts about the body and disease and on the basis of that technical knowledge does something for a *person*. In that sense it can be seen in the same light as any moral behavior—moral because it has directly to do with the welfare and the good of others. Morality deals with the right and the wrong, with the good and the bad. Still, the nature of the moral sphere is difficult to define and the dictionary is of little help. The word "morality" has been used as a bridge between ethics—"the ought"—and conduct —"the is." In the practice of medicine, we might say, the doctor keeps before him a body "ought" and a body "is." Presumably, in health the "ought" and "is" of the body are the same, while in sickness they are different.

It might be argued that speaking of "ought" and "is" in the context of the facts about the body and disease is a misuse of the term "morality," a confusion of facts and values: the doctor is dealing with facts (at least as he sees his function), and the body "ought" is not an ethic but a fact. One might say, to point up that confusion, that a plumber works the same way in repairing a leak or installing a sink, that the plumber has an "ought" and an "is" for pipes and that therefore his behavior in relation to the pipes can be examined in moral terms. While plumbers certainly can be immoral, commonly we would say that they can be immoral only in relation to *people*, not pipes. To the pipes, which are inanimate, unfeeling, replaceable, and fixable in six different ways, the plumber cannot be immoral. He can merely do a good or a bad job.

Thus the analogy of the plumber would show us that the body "ought" and "is" are in the realm of fact, not value, *only if we could compare bodies to pipes*. We cannot, and hence we are offended when we see doctors treating bodies like pipes rather than persons. It is, actually, quite possible to conceive of a body like a piece of cast-iron pipe; perhaps such a concept is even necessary to understanding the body, but it is only partially useful to medical care. It is the doctors' caring function we are speaking about when we discuss what right they have to make ethical decisions for their patients.

In the care of the sick the doctor is confronted with a body "ought" and a body "is," and he applies his skills in an attempt to make the two conform. But the doctor confronted with the "ought" and the "is" of a person is dealing with that person's welfare, which can be seen only in ethical or moral terms. Thus even when a physician claims not to be engaged in moral behavior when caring for the sick, the fact that disease resides in persons makes a disregard of the moral and of human values in itself a kind of inhumane behavior. The conflicting needs of the patient's self and body are often present in even the mildest illness.

Take, for example, a twenty-eight-year-old actor who has just landed his first important movie role when he develops a nonspecific illness resembling a bad cold. He continues working and develops severe chest pain which on examination is diagnosed as a kind of viral pleurisy. With rest, a patient with this illness usually gets better quickly; but if he continues working, the infection will persist and may severely worsen, even possibly (but rarely) becoming life-threatening. What is the doctor's job? In *body terms* the answer is clear. He informs the actor of all the possible consequences and insists that he go to bed to ensure that the illness is cured (with the coincidental result that the actor will lose his job). In *person terms* he helps assess the relative risks and agrees to continue to act as arbiter between the actor's desires and the needs of his body, and in so doing takes on responsibility for the risks incurred.

Another example is the patient who calls to say that yesterday she injured her back lifting a heavy suitcase and tomorrow she has to drive several hundred miles to visit her children in camp. The body valuation—estimating the nature and degree of injury to the back—is clearly seen to be part of the physician's function in making a diagnosis. In instances of this sort, which occur many times a day, more is asked of the doctor. He must measure and weigh against the body valuation a set of personal considerations. ("Beverly, why can't you visit your children next weekend?" "But this is the camp's only visiting weekend for parents!") It might be argued that such personal considerations are none of the physician's business and that his job is merely to make the diagnosis and to give body information when asked, rather like giving a stock market quotation. It is difficult to conceive of a patient who would be satisfied, or even well served, by a doctor who had such a limited concept of his job.

The physician is not making the decision for the patient. He is acting as consultant to an adult who needs information. But for the information to be useful, the doctor must understand the concerns of the patient—understand not only what the question is, but as far as possible what the question means.

In the complex equation created in illness by the

needs of person, body, and society, physicians play a vital role. As the only ones who know the body (it does not matter if their body knowledge is correct, only that it is culturally consonant), they are the ones who can legitimate body demands. Thus the doctor is the arbiter between the person and his body and, as has been made clear by the sociologists of medicine, also a representative of society and its values.

Still another example to help clarify the point: A fifty-seven-year-old businessman was seen in the emergency room of a New York City hospital with chest pain that was uncharacteristic but suggested the possibility of a heart attack. None of the clinical findings, including the electrocardiogram, confirmed the diagnosis, but the physician, troubled by the story of the pain, advised hospitalization. The man said that that would be difficult, since he lived in Maryland. The doctor, who had a picture in his mind of the patient's dying on the Metroliner on his way home, said, "Earl, I don't care where you live; I really think it would be wisest to stay in the hospital until we sort this thing out. I don't think you should take the chance of something happening." So the patient stayed and indeed, as later tests showed, he had suffered a heart attack.

But let us suppose that, when told he ought to stay in the hospital, the patient said, "Doctor, I can't do that. I have to go home; my wife is sick and all alone." The doctor would then ask, "What's the matter with your wife?" It may seem a natural question, but it has nothing to do with the diagnostic problem of whether the patient has had a heart attack. If the patient answered that the wife had the "flu," the doctor would say, "Come on, Earl, your wife will get over the flu without you, if necessary."

If, on the other hand, the man said, "Doc, I can't stay here. I *must* go home; today I got a call from my wife's doctor, and he said she's dying!" the situation would change. The physician would now have to take into account the wife's condition as well as her husband's condition because *both* are part of the patient's condition. Such medical decisions are particularly difficult because of the probabilistic nature of the events involved. The doctor doesn't *know* that the man is having a heart attack; he only considers it a real probability, based on his experience and judgment. But what if the patient were kept in the hospital and did *not* have a heart attack and the wife died in his absence? The patient would feel terribly guilty and partly responsible for the wife's death, and the doctor would share those feelings.

We can make one other change in the anecdote. Suppose that while the patient is talking about his dying wife, his chest pain increases, he becomes pale and sweaty, and he goes into shock. Now there is no question of what must be done. The doctor must save the man's life no matter what happens to the wife. The man is his patient, and in this situation the man's life is the doctor's primary responsibility.

Here, clearly, moral issues are involved. The physician who refused to take into account personal considerations such as the dying wife would be considered merely a technician by the same people who criticize him for making moral decisions at such high levels as when to turn off the respirator. On the other hand, the physician who took only the personal into account would be remiss in his obligations to the body.

The anecdote makes it obvious that the implications

of the most routine, seemingly innocuous decisions inevitably lead to the deepest ethical issues. It is these profound questions, and our unease about how physicians handle them, that compels us to doubt the physician's ethical prerogatives, our doubts arising, in part, because we know how fallible all men are.

Too often ethical problems in medicine are discussed as though the decision in question occupied no more than a moment in time, an instantaneous event involving merely the physician. While this may be true in the sense that every decision does occupy only a moment in time when it becomes an actuality—for example, writing an order on a hospital chart or making the decision to resuscitate a patient whose heart has stopped—such decisions are only the end of a continuum that may have occupied hours, days, months, or even years. *To reflect only on the decision itself is to negate the importance of the continuum.*

Medical care is a *process*. It cannot be seen or even discussed as a single incident, as one static decision made on a static set of facts. In the *process of care*, especially in cases that eventually demand difficult moral decisions, a number of minor ethical matters have been handled along the way—matters that involve both fact and value, in which both patient and doctor interact in making decisions. In that process both patient and physician have informed each other of how each feels, and the interaction helps form the basis for the next decision. It is important to realize that, in the handling of a case, the physician has made many ethical decisions respecting his patient, in full view of the patient and usually with the patient's consent.

In discussing such monumental moral problems as "allowing to die," "turning off the respirator," and choosing to administer "extraordinary treatment," the features of individual cases that lead to the crucial decision are lost. This may be appropriate, even necessary, in order to arrive at universal principles or general statements about bio-ethics, but it obscures the complexities inherent in the doctor-patient relationship, which are vital to understanding moral problems in medicine.

It would be misleading to insist that in each individual case a dialogue between patient and doctor is inevitably present because that is not true. Some patients meet their physicians only at the moment of death or on admission to the hospital with their fatal illness, but others have known their doctors for years. In such long-term relationships not only is each patient a person to the doctor, but he is a person to his patients. Some physicians are more insensitive or farther removed from their patients than others, and some settings are more conducive to such a process than others. But in a normally paced relationship the patient and doctor inform each other through time as to how they feel about such situations as painful lingering or telling the whole truth to the patient. Sometimes the information is transmitted by direct conversation about the problem. The patient, healthy at the time, may say, "If I ever have cancer, don't you tell me; I couldn't bear it," or, "I want to know the truth, no matter how awful." Sometimes the discussion takes place at the time the problem arises; but even then, although the conversation may be complete, we would fail to appreciate the process if we considered the discussion to be whole in itself.

The process often starts before the patient ever sees the doctor. One seldom chooses his or her physician blindly from the Yellow Pages of the telephone book. Usually one finds out about a doctor from family or friends and learns ahead of time not only how competent the physician is, but also through anecdote and otherwise what kind of person he or she is, how much he or she cares, and so forth. At the time of the first visit those impressions are reinforced, sometimes deliberately by a probing patient and sometimes without awareness in idle conversation. In these conversations the patient somehow manages to convey to the physician his or her beliefs about the body, life, fate, sickness, and death, probably without ever actually discussing those topics; and the doctor, I believe, responds in kind.

The first visit often establishes whether or not doctor and patient share similar values. (If not, the patient rarely returns.) More important, perhaps, the first visit also establishes whether or not the doctor understands the patient.

The major complaint people have about their doctors is that they don't listen. Listening means hearing not only what the symptoms are but what they mean to the patient. Understanding means not only understanding the words but also understanding, in the sense of being sympathetic to, the values that are behind the words. When medicine is conceived as a purely technological field, learning how to listen to these personal aspects of the patient's concern may not be considered part of the doctor's professional role by other professionals. As one dermatologist said to me, he thought of his "bedside manner" as just something he had to pick up in order to have a successful practice. That his personal understanding was often vital to making his patients better was not within his comprehension.

The importance of shared or mutually understood values is also underscored by the previously cited case of the man who had a chest pain in New York and whose wife was in Maryland. Remember that I suggested as an alternative scenario that the patient said he must return home because his wife was dying. The moral dilemma is posed for the doctor not only because of the patient's desire to go home but because the doctor is aware of the importance of obligations to family and the possible depth of the bond between husband and wife. These things the physician learns merely as part of his total life experience, but here again that experience is essential to the humane performance of his medical functions. He learns these things best when he has respect for the importance of his life experience in directing his decisions regarding his patients.

In certain ways the physician learns what life is really about underneath the social conventions. He experiences life and people at their worst—in pain and sorrow and bereft of dignity. But he is also granted the privilege of seeing in his patients courage and acceptance, resignation and determination—of participating in the life crises inherent in the human condition that test the character and the souls of men and women. As his knowledge increases, what he has learned must enter his decisions; the depth and richness of his experience must temper his technological skill.

Though largely irrelevant to the healthy, the doctor's day-to-day work is concerned with events that may occur only once or twice in his patient's lifetime. A baby's birth may be routine to him, but for the mother those hours of labor may be the proving ground of adulthood. His simple common-sense advice about the breast and breast-feeding rescues a mother from what seemed to her to be her own failure. That man's drinking, this child's height, another's sexual dysfunction—all vital problems to those concerned —are influenced by his words. The doctor is in and out of the lives of others. Where serious or terminal illness is the issue, he may become a family intimate for days, weeks, or months, again becoming external to their lives when trouble ends. From his unique perspective he watches people and their families grow, some members maturing, others dying, all simultaneously with the growth of his own family; his own life provides the touchstone of empathy from which he observes his patients and hears what they tell him.

It should be clearer now why the interchange between physician and patient or between physician and the patient's family is so important in the process of making moral decisions and why such decisions are an inescapable part of the physician's work.

Two days after I had canceled the old man's ampicillin in the case cited at the beginning of this chapter, I asked the intern why she had treated the patient's pneumonia. In our discussion of the clinical problem we shared a common language and syntax and a common understanding of the pathology and process. But when I suggested that it would have been better *not* to have started antibiotics— that it was one of her functions as a physician to allow a graceful death—our mutual comprehension ceased. We understood each other as long as our conversation was restricted to the patient's disease. We stumbled and failed when we tried to discuss those subjective elements that should have entered the treatment decision. Both of us knew of the family's desire that the patient undergo no undue distress. Both of us had feelings about how we should like death to come to us and to those close to us. But these common understandings did not appear to be part of our shared *professional* interest; rather, they seemed to be only a private matter. She had not been trained to understand that these things were part of her professional concern. That lack of training is not her fault.

Let me underline the problem with another example. Assembled at a teaching conference I conducted at a hospital in New York City were a dozen interns and residents with the most diverse cultural backgrounds—French, Taiwanese, Swiss, Pakistani, Philippine, Yugoslav, and American—discussing a problem that troubled them. A man in his nineties had been found lying in Pennsylvania Station and had been brought into the hospital's emergency room. Initially, his moribund condition seemed to result from malnutrition. Within a few days, however, the story emerged: he had been confined to a state mental institution for more than twenty-five years and less than a month previously had escaped to freedom (to his joy).

He flourished on the ward, but routine blood tests revealed that he had an anemia, and as careful physicians the doctors searched for its cause and discovered a tumor of the stomach. The question raised was how vigorously they should pursue the exact diagnosis of the tumor (which, in itself, was not very large—nor was it causing him any distress). Angiography, biopsy, and other procedures were suggested. They seemed unanimous in the need to press on, although they were by no means unanimous about whether they would want to do definitive surgery once the tumor was defined. I was so struck by their scientific unanimity in the face of a literal United Nations of represented cultures that I asked them to consider the procedure in relation to how they felt about the old man himself and what they thought should be done for him. We all became interested and, from the lively discussion that followed, one thing was clear: no matter what they felt privately or would do for a friend or a member of their own family, in the hospital setting one culture was dominant over all the others—the culture of scientific medicine.

Both of these cases show young, scientifically trained doctors in the pursuit of disease. Both cases illustrate the doctor as curer rather than as healer, and in both cases the scientific mode of thinking has driven out the humanist mode of thinking about their patients from humane doctors in training.

Why should scientific-technological thinking appear to be in competition with (and, in fact, win out over) the humanist mode of thought? The roots of the problem can be found in the fact that physicians are trained to think in a manner that elevates questions of disease, phrased in a scientific way, over other questions raised by human illness.

It is essential to realize that technology in itself did not create the problems in these two cases. Modern technological medicine is a wonderful thing—for you, for me, and for my patients. I don't very often stand at a bedside and say that there is nothing I can do. I may not be able to cure or offer a return to life, but I can almost always *do something* (or do nothing constructively; the choice is there). I do not want to return to the "old days" (even a few years back) or stop technological advances. The solution to our problems is not to deny technology or to pretend that it is unnecessary. A doctor must maintain his technological mastery or he will practice poor medicine. Other approaches to sickness can supplement, enrich, or extend technical knowledge, but nothing can replace it.

One of the reasons the doctors with such different cultural backgrounds all had similar points of view is that technological medicine works—and works better than anything the profession has ever had before. The scientifically trained physician is very much more effective than his less-well-trained colleague. (In the endless discussion of the scientific versus the "humanist" physician, the question is usually asked whether one would rather be taken care of by someone who knew his technology well or by someone who just gave loving care. What is not clear is why the two are considered to be in opposition to each other. In the proposition as given I would rather have the scientific doctor. But again, why must I choose as though one excluded the other?)

But the clear-cut power of technological medicine does not win the competition between curing and healing solely through its effectiveness *because it also wins where it is inappropriate and ineffective*, as in the treatment of those two failed old men.

Another reason why the scientific mode wins out in the care of patients, often to the detriment of their human needs, is based on a certain natural circularity of thought. That is to say, scientific medicine deals with disease; its view of the world of the sick is the view of disease. The manner in which physicians are trained quite naturally emphasizes and reinforces the current definitions of disease and the view of illness that such definitions promote, and their education stresses the rational analytic thought of science. Analytic thinking, which is so useful to physicians in understanding the body, leads away from considerations of the whole person and is in conflict with that within the doctor which would be more useful for his healing function.

In the course of his training the medical student for the first time approaches the body as an object—a body completely depersonalized, stripped of those awesome aspects that constitute the unique nature of individuals. He is confronted instead with the awesomeness of the body as a complicated biological machine. In anatomy the student takes the body apart muscle by muscle, nerve by nerve, and organ by organ, and learns to understand it (in theory at least) by knowing how the whole is constructed. He is taught that to really understand how the body functions, he must see it not as a collection of individual pieces but as integrated systems. Nonetheless, the first step to integrated knowledge is disintegration. The same process is repeated in biochemistry and physiology, where the functions of the body are examined in all their minute and fascinating detail.

While learning the facts of these sciences and the mode of scientific thinking, the student gradually learns to think biologically—to consider the human in bodily, rather than personal, terms. In order to keep medical students from becoming too one-sided, most good medical schools attempt to show the relevance of the basic sciences to the care of patients. In addition, the curriculum usually includes courses designed to speak of the wider world of medicine and society. Despite the fact that these classes really "turn on" the student, it is the sciences that get the greatest attention and scientific thinking that is most valued.

Thus, throughout their first year in medical school the students have been submerged in a way of thought whose utility has been clearly demonstrated. Furthermore, the logic of the body and of biological systems has started to become their logic.

During the second year of medical school, in pathology, bacteriology (including immunology), and biostatistics, the students are immersed in modern concepts of disease causality. As they peer through microscopes at slides of diseased organs, they are seeing the cell theory of disease. Through their study of pathology in conjunction with the biochemistry and pathophysiology of disease, elucidated during this century, they now define disease as do their teachers and the whole culture of scientific medicine. In microbiology they are exposed to the basic model of causality in disease: for each disease, there is a cause. Though increased sophistication has led to modifications of the older belief in one-cause-one-disease to account for such concepts as multifactor causality, the underlying philosophy of cause remains the same.

As the students enter their third year, they are ready to participate in the care of patients. They have acquired a world view and the mode of thought that produced that view. They have learned a special language that at once reveals their knowledge of the new world but at the same time locks them into the mode of thought and the special picture of that world. For them to attempt to use another thought mode or to explore alternative constructions of reality would threaten the still shaky foundations of their new knowledge—a knowledge whose success and efficacy seem proved on all sides. In the light of all this, is it any wonder that in the case cited earlier those young physicians from such different backgrounds all approached the problem of the old man with the stomach tumor in the same way? Despite the many different countries in which they received their medical education, they were all trained in essentially the same manner as the American student (at least at some point of their schooling).

The educational process I have just described is a potent force for maintaining the new doctor within the analytic thought system of science and for excluding as nonprofessional other views of the world of the sick or other ways of thinking about patients, despite the fact that physicians do not think that way about themselves or those close to them. I reiterate the point because, as I explore the professional thinking of physicians, the reader must constantly be aware that alternative modes of thought are available. We are aware of the relativity of our perception of the world. We know that our unconscious—our inner needs, drives, and conflicts—has an effect on what we see or hear and how we interpret those perceptions. Similarly, education and the field in which we are trained mold the way we see reality: sociologists, experimental psychologists, and psychiatrists viewing the same phenomenon may interpret it in vastly different ways. Each uses the same analytic thought mode but uses different methods and different basic concepts to examine the phenomenon. The scientific method employed by a discipline to examine some particular event determines in large part how it will appear to the investigator.

As mentioned earlier, the special world view that physicians acquire is based on the analytic thought in which they were trained. That is only a partial explanation of the world view just as the analytic thought mode of science is only part of the thinking processes of physicians (or of anyone else, for that matter).

The other type of thought that helps construct the physician's world is valuational thinking, the mode of thought that maintains one's conceptions. A conception of something is the way it is defined in the mind—what it means in the fullest sense, in terms not only of words but also of feeling, beliefs, and images.

Conceptions do not, so to speak, float around freely in the mind. As willow trees are related to other trees and trees are related to forests, so conceptions are related to one another. Through the relationships between conceptions, belief structures are built that determine how people see and interpret the world. One could even say that they *are* the world for each of us.

As the medical student progresses through his training, he is given a whole new set of conceptions about the body, about diseases, about doctors, hospitals, and so forth. Some are taught specifically, as with the conceptions of the specific diseases; and some are learned by precedent, as with the conceptions of the role of physicians. As the years go by, the whole medical system is taught and the student learns a belief structure for medicine.

It may seem that I have been inconsistent. Earlier I said that the student in the course of his medical education was *taught* the analytic thought mode of science, but now I have suggested that he *learns* the whole interrelated set of conceptions that make up the medical world view. Those are part of valuational thought. The inconsistency is resolved, I think, by showing how the two are interdependent; how each is enriched; and finally, it appears to me, how analytic thought in the doctor's training has driven valuational thought from view.

If a physician tells us that a particular patient has pneumonia, he can justify his diagnosis by analyzing the case for us, explaining the manifestations of the disease in the most detailed scientific terms. But each step in the explanation would be an analytic statement that rational-

izes or explains the features of the concept "pneumonia."
While such statements may be "true" and necessary for
real understanding of pneumonia, their value to the clinical
physician who cares for patients is dependent on the existing conception of pneumonia. There is no way to take the
entire series of relevant analytic statements and recompile
them to arrive at the conception "pneumonia" in any but
its barest outlines (if at all). The conception is the organizing unit, and testing its validity—does this or that feature
rightfully belong?—is one of the vital functions that analytic thought plays in the conception's maintenance.

Let us see how each kind of thinking is enriched.
Analytic thinking is enhanced by following each finding
to the necessary underlying conclusions. Each step is fascinating in itself and builds a fabric of knowledge that is
also fascinating, but it leads ever farther away from the
person in whom the disease occurred. More wonderful is
the way the physician can make explicit each step in the
reasoning process. By doing so, he excites the interest of
the students and they, too, join the pursuit as each answer
produces another question. The richness lies in the details
open to all who will inquire and in the developed pattern
with the answer to so many questions in a life beset by
questions. Little does it matter that the answers are to
questions that seldom trouble physicians when they wonder
about themselves and their lives.

Richness in valuational thought lies in another direction. There it is the investment of each conception with
greater detail as experience finds existing detail wanting.
In medicine, at least, each new experience means another
encounter with a specific disease and, consequently, with
a person who has the disease. How can the features of the

diseases be disentangled from the people who contained them? Commonly one hears physicians speak of a case: "I once had a case like this: when I was in the Army, there was a sergeant who . . ." In the recitation a person is described as part of the case. Each case is unique, and gradually so is each doctor's conception of the disease. The good physician learns to disentangle the elements of his thought, but they remain, in part, unique to him. There can be no pretense of universality of experience here, as in the demonstrations of analytic thinking.

Moreover, each doctor brings to his observations something of himself. Were two physicians to see the same patient at the same time, they would enlarge their conception of the patient's disease in different ways. These differences are the essence of the subjective. But physicians have been trained in medicine to believe that subjectivity is the enemy of science—even of truth. So subjectivity is suppressed, at least for public consumption, since it runs counter to the public faith. In this manner, one kind of thinking (analytic-scientific) drives the other (valuational-conceptual) into hiding. Thus is lost the opportunity to actively teach physicians in training a disciplined mode of thought that is clearly an essential part of clinical medicine.

The young physician has within his head an encyclopedia of related conceptions of diseases, symptoms, causes, and relationships, as well as a manifest thought mode with which to operate on these conceptions. In the beginning these conceptions are a product of didactic learning, but soon experience begins to add to the learned conceptions. It is the great advantage of the American system of bedside teaching that the student can enrich his didactic conceptions by exposure to the reality of sick patients early in the training. Nonetheless, it is apparent that in applying his training to the care of the sick, the physician will from almost the first tend to "see what he knows": to make reality conform to his conceptions rather than enlarge his conceptions when they do not conform to the perceived experience. After all, we are not speaking simply of one single conception but of a whole system of interrelated conceptions. If key conceptions are threatened by a perception at odds with them, the whole system or network is threatened. Even in their later years, we find physicians whose conceptions remain undisturbed by a reality completely contradictory to them—from whence comes the aphorism about a doctor in practice for twenty years: that he has not had twenty years' experience but only one year's experience twenty times.

In practice, the application of conceptual thought may be seen in the search for the diagnosis. Some medical students were asked why they wanted to do a particular arduous diagnostic procedure on their patient. One of them answered that their chief resident had said that only three things were important in medicine: "The diagnosis, the diagnosis, and the diagnosis." While the story may be apocryphal, it illustrates a common medical attitude, particularly in the idealized setting represented by the university teaching hospital. In any particular patient the search for a diagnosis may acquire a life of its own, and in working toward that diagnosis, the patient's original complaints, life situation, needs, fears, and economics may become irrelevant. The scenario is directed more by available technology, the special interests of the personnel, the schedules of the institution, and above all, the hidden nature of the disease, which must be found because, like Mount Everest, "it is there." There is among physicians a compelling need to know what is wrong, for it is around the categorization of disease that the whole system of modern medicine is organized. Central to everything else is the concept of disease whose evolution we have already traced: that alterations in tissue structure can be found to account for all alterations in function. (Consider the constant search for alterations in the brain to explain psychiatric disorders.) In recent years this basic concept has been enlarged to include biochemical or genetic alterations on a par with structural alterations, but the concept remains central. Physiology, biochemistry, and immunology provide explanations for disease in the service of the basic concept. The explanations of disease that make up the medical paradigm are, so to speak, the fixed navigating platforms of medicine from which everything else is oriented.

The utility of the basic concept of disease should not be underestimated. Not only did it bring order to the understanding of the sick but also to the development of therapy. When physicians could agree on common definitions of disease, it became possible to compare the effectiveness of therapy in a systematic manner. More could be said to show the tremendous importance of shared, stable basic conceptions. But our purpose here is rather to show how the physician may be unable to "see" those aspects of the sick that do not fit the conceptual system.

At issue is a category of human experience that has been systematically excluded from the purview of physicians during the development and scientization of modern medicine. Consequently, no method exists for making the appropriate nonmedical "diagnosis" (fitting to a conception within the larger system of modern medicine), and there is no traditional recipe to solve the "nonmedical" problems the sick present. There are, as we shall see, non-traditional, latent, or covert solutions that physicians employ unconsciously and that inevitably arise from their status as physicians and the role assigned to them as doctors.

Let us return to the young intern who treated the pneumonia of the old man with the stroke, instead of allowing him to die a peaceful death, and to the house staff who, despite their widely differing cultural backgrounds, were unanimous in depersonalizing the case of the old man with the stomach tumor. The system of medical thought in which they had been trained did not include as part of their *professional concern* aspects of either case that fell outside conceptions of disease. They had been trained in analytic thought, a system of thought that seems inappropriate to a consideration of the humane aspects of decisions. The analytic mode of thought—the mechanics of scientific thinking—works well in the service of a complex system of interrelated conceptions that deal with the structure of the body and its alteration in disease. Doctors are trained to search out the evidence of the disease presented by the sick. They know how to analyze the evidence, to weigh and rank it, to define the clinical problem, develop solutions, and make rapid or thoughtful decisions, all based on the system and supported by the most sophisticated science and technology.

But if the central problem in the case lies outside those areas for which the system of medicine has conceptions or falls within categories that are evaluated lower, the central problem (such as what to do with the old man who escaped from the mental hospital) ceases to be a

medical matter, becoming instead "social," "psychological," or "personal" and no longer within the province of
doctors.

However, as I showed earlier, problems that do fall
within the system of medicine are *also* moral matters because medical decisions affect not only the body but also
the life and welfare of the patient. Perhaps that would
not be so if in each case there was only one right decision
or only one correct course of action, but in medicine there
are frequently several possible courses of action, each of
which is technically correct. Or there may be only one
technically proper decision but several different ways of
implementing it, each of which would affect the life of the
patient somewhat differently.

I hope you now agree that doctors *do* make moral
decisions, and that it would seem that these moral decisions are an inherent and inescapable part of the physician's work. Furthermore, it seems evident that doctors
have not simply taken this function on themselves. It is
not just a "generalization of expertise"—that because they
are proficient in dealing with the technical aspects, they
assume that they can deal well with the moral issues. Socially, assigning this responsibility to physicians is extremely useful. The sick are weak, and in their weakness,
which may be shared by their loved ones, judgment is impaired by emotion. We say that the sick person is distracted
by his illness, pain, or disability and is unable to bring his
"full capacity" to bear on a decision. In fact the impair-
ment is qualitative, a shift from the primarily "rational"
to the primarily emotive thought in decision-making.
Since it is difficult to know, in ourselves, when judgment is
rational or emotive, how useful for the sick to have a group

within society to turn to and hand over the responsibility for maintaining rational processes.

In the empathy-objectivity battle within the physician, we all expect—even demand—that his judgments remain based on rational process. Similarly, with moral decisions we expect rational thinking of the physician. The question is no longer where physicians get the right to make moral decisions; society and individual patients thrust that responsibility on them. What do doctors do to protect themselves from the painful consequences of the responsibility that goes with the right to make such decisions?

The responsibility is awesome—and impossible, too great a burden to bear. It is terrifying for the physician to conceive that something he does, even some little thing, will destroy a life, adversely alter a family, ruin happiness, or produce anything except salutary change. It is a conception from which physicians, like all other people, must protect themselves. Who could function under such a burden if it were in full view? Conversely, what person can give himself over to the care of another, knowing the dangers and also knowing, as we all do, the frailties of men?

The simplest protection of all is the insistent belief that it is not true: The physician does not make ethical decisions; he makes technical decisions.

Recently, in discussing the death from heart attack of a famous and beloved athlete, I said I was happy his death had taken that form. At the time of his death he was living with the threat of blindness or of the loss of his legs, or both, within relatively few months. These alternatives seemed particularly awful for this active and powerful man. Another doctor present, a medical researcher, said, "How can you say that? You're playing God!" I had made no decision that caused death in preference to the other outcomes. What did he mean?

"Playing God,"—an odd accusation that is hurled at doctors from medical-school days to, I suspect, old age. It has recently become clear to me what the phrase really means: "Playing God" means making a nontechnical decision—a moral decision. I have always wondered what it meant, since, in the situations in which it is so often used, it has been hard to see how one decision is more "playing God" than another. To use a classic example: A patient with terminal cancer is clearly dying. The disease is widespread and overwhelming, and the patient is within days of death. Blood tests show an increasing, and now severe, anemia. The intern suggests blood transfusions and the resident refuses. The intern and the medical students say that the resident is "playing God." If the transfusions are given, the patient may live a short while longer. Why is denying the transfusion any more "playing God" than giving the transfusion, since, in giving the blood, life will be extended? Extending life is seemingly as much "playing God" as denying life. It is clear, however, that giving the blood is a technical decision based on tests or other technical assessments of the case. Withholding the blood has no technical basis. *Withholding is a moral decision.* The resident then defends himself by pointing out that blood is in short supply and better used in a case with a more hopeful outcome. The assignment of priority is, again, a "technical," not a moral, decision and is approved grudgingly by the students and the interns as they learn to assign priorities to their work. With a technical rationale, the resident is no longer "playing God."

The historical roots of the problem can be traced back to Descartes's mind-body duality, which was also effectively a moral-technical duality: physicians, in company with other scientists, were given the (technical) body, while philosophers and theologians were assigned the (moral) mind. Obviously this controversy has not cooled. At issue is the degree to which the mind-self-soul is part of the human machine, and therefore understandable in the terms that define that machine. That part not understandable in scientific (machine) terms is involved with values and morals.

Physicians are clearly involved in the care of the machine. They make technical decisions based on their understanding of the body and its malfunctions. Pragmatically, they remain out of the area of morality and philosophy, except as regards certain standards of behavior that are expected of them and that are discussed in moral terms. This morality involves their interaction with patients and other physicians, but it does not define what their behavior should be concerning moral decisions about their patients' lives; it does not define for them, except in the most general terms (i.e., saving life), how they are to make ethical decisions that concern the patient.

The Code of Ethics of Sir Thomas Percival, written in 1773, is explicit in many areas of the behavior of physicians, but not in regard to moral decision-making about patients. It does, however, require that the ideal physician adhere to a strict code of personal behavior. As with other medical oaths and codes, it is consistently demanded of the physician that he lead an exemplary moral existence. The underlying assumption is that following those precepts will result in an ethical man or woman who, it is presumed, will make "proper" judgments.

Now we are at a time when the moral problems that face physicians are increasingly difficult. Pretending that they are not there will not make them go away. Our defenses against the knowledge that physicians make moral judgments have worked so well that we are now more endangered by the defense than by the original problem.

The old conception of the mind-body conflict has outlived its utility. Though science has won its battle with the church, the conflict is still keeping us from achieving a unity between mind and body, between the treatment of persons and the treatment of diseases. Perhaps its most damaging effect for our life as a society is that the conflict, in its modern continuance, becomes a contest between the technical and the moral. No longer a struggle between science and the church where science must triumph for mankind to progress, the victory of science has converted the struggle between the technical and the moral into an attempt to provide technical solutions to what are inherently moral problems.

We are familiar with such technical solutions to moral problems in medicine, most particularly in the case of the dying. Death becomes a technical matter, a failure of technology to rescue the body from a threat to its functioning and integrity. It does not matter that the death of a person cannot be removed from the moral order, from the bonds of conscience, sentiment, and morality that describe what is right. What matters is the mythology of the society, the widespread belief that things essentially moral can be made technical.

Since the physician deals directly with the welfare of individuals, medicine must be recognized as a moral profession whose tools are, in part, technical. I say in part, rather than entirely, technical because one of the most important tools of medicine is the person of the physician himself. Medicine is concerned with the care of persons *by* persons, as simple as that.

While it may seem obvious to us that medicine is devoted to the care of persons, the tendencies in the history of medicine that contributed to the separateness of the person from his disease give us some insight into the reasons why the truism "treat the patient as a whole person" remains a truism more honored in the breach than in the fulfillment. The entire thrust of medical history, to say nothing of current practice and technological power, mitigates against medicine, as a profession, seeing its mission primarily in terms of persons. Moreover, it does not matter that physicians *think* they are primarily engaged in the care of diseases. They are involved in the lives of other persons, making decisions that are inherently moral and that are dependent on the nature of the person they are treating.

Though it is clear that medicine concerns itself with persons who are sick, rather than merely with their diseases, it is not at all clear what we mean by the notion of person. It may seem odd to raise a question about the meaning of the concept of person, since we all know intuitively what we mean by the word. But intuition is not sufficient if we want the person of the patient to assume a far greater importance in the teaching of medicine and medical practice. We have already seen that, whether he knows it or not, the physician, whenever possible, does draw upon his knowledge of the patient as a person in his decision-making process (and vice versa). But where the assessment of the disease state is an open and manifest part of his job as a doctor, the assessment of the patient as a person is often a latent or an unacknowledged part of the physician's function. As such, the doctor's skill comes not from specific training but from increasing experience with people and the world. He is in that regard very much like anyone else except that his work requires him to sharpen his perceptions and quicken his intuitions if his decisions are to be well made. Indeed, older, experienced physicians become very efficient at sizing up people rapidly from minimal cues. But if we were to ask them what they mean by the word "person"—just what a person is—they would have the same difficulties of definition the rest of us have.

The problem, of course, is not new. Perhaps by definition and almost certainly by general agreement, the nature of person is central to notions of ethics and morality. What a man is and what a man ought to do are queries that revolve around the general question of the nature of man. And yet, although philosophers have struggled with these issues for thousands of years, precise understanding remains elusive. We see this in medicine in discussions about when to turn off the respirator or whether certain malformed infants should be allowed to die. The decisions pivot on the question of when someone becomes human or when he loses his humanness. Some moral philosophers have attempted to formulate lists of those attributes that make us persons. Self-awareness, the capacity to relate to others, intelligence, and many other factors have been advanced as essential parts of being human. But when I read these discussions, I do not find the guidance I need for making difficult ethical decisions at the bedside. The very fact of all the current interest in these matters, however, does serve to emphasize how important and relevant the issue of personhood is to a decision made at the bedside.

But what better guidelines to the nature of person are there than the philosophers' lists of attributes or the experienced doctors' intuition? There appear to be none. You may argue that modern psychiatry based on Freud's great discoveries does provide us with the understanding of persons we need. While I do not question the vast increase in our knowledge of human psychology that has followed Freud's original contributions, we still do not know how to define a person.

It is necessary to make a distinction between the particulars of personhood and the psychology of a person, since the term "psychology" is now used so widely as to have lost virtually all meaning. The following example may help to show the effect on medicine of a nearly universal psychologism among doctors and students (and perhaps everybody else).

A young man of twenty-five had difficulty in swallowing and pain in his throat of unusual character and duration, which worried him greatly. He saw several physicians over a period of a few months and was treated without effect. No specific disease was found, but he was not reassured. An adequate history revealed that his father had died six months earlier of cancer of the esophagus. Further questions showed that he was the only unmarried child and still lived at home with his mother. Armed with these facts and with the results of an examination that confirmed the absence of disease, the doctors were able to reassure him.

When the case was related to some medical students, one of them said that she thought the patient probably had the symptoms because he felt guilty over the father's death and the fact that he had won the Oedipal battle. Indeed, the student could have been correct. But she leaped over the patient's expressed sense of responsibility to his mother directly to the interpretation. Leaping over the observation to the interpretation is a particularly common error in these days of psychological sophistication. The result is that we have come to know a great deal about the underlying mechanisms of behavioral disorders but remarkably little about such normal human characteristics as the sense of responsibility.

This is not to belittle the importance of such interpretations as guilt associated with Oedipal conflict but only to point out that a sense of responsibility seems to be a universal characteristic of humans (we would certainly consider its total absence strange, if not pathological), a characteristic that is pertinent to moral decisions—those concerning the welfare of others.

I take the sense of responsibility to be part of the anatomy of a person just as the gallbladder is part of the anatomy of the body; that is, a sense of responsibility, the ability to form relationships, curiosity, the need for control, the need to be loved and to be needed, embarrassment, shame, dignity, honor, and many other attributes are all universally found among persons to a varying degree and in varying manifestations.

No psychological system of which I am aware explains the presence of these properties in persons. A psychology may tell us how they develop, why one enlarges and another atrophies, or even the pathology that develops when one of those factors is absent. Psychologies may even tell us why they are present in the teleological sense that it is good for persons to have those qualities, but nothing explains why they are there; they are simply part of the moral biology of mankind. It seems strange to me as I

write this because I, too, am so used to psychological interpretations. Odd, because I have no trouble distinguishing
between an acknowledgment of the anatomical presence of
the gallbladder and an understanding of its evolution,
embryology, physiology, and pathology. Yet those particular qualities of person are absolutely pertinent to decisions about the care of patients.

Suppose, for example, in the case cited above the
young man *was* found to have a cancer of the esophagus.
Now, although the possibility of guilt secondary to unresolved Oedipal conflict remains important to know and
even act on, we are aware that the young man's feeling of
responsibility for his mother is also important. That is, in
making decisions about his treatment we must take into
account his desire that the mother's needs be met; otherwise, we shall have failed to meet the needs of the patient
as a person. I am emphasizing here the particulars of
person because they are so little studied and understood
while psychological mechanisms are so well known and
even overused (or misused).

One problem in understanding the nature of person is
that the elements of a person are different from the elements of the gallbladder or even of the unconscious. The
properties of a person are not like the properties of a rec-
tangle. Indeed, the properties of a person are not even like
the properties of the heart. We know precisely what we
mean by blood flow, systole, diastole, ventricular muscle,
and so on. The meanings of these things do not change
from heart to heart. But the meanings of self-awareness,
sense of responsibility, dignity, and so on are of a very different kind. They change from individual to individual.
Furthermore, the shape the sense of responsibility takes in

that patient is itself undergoing continuous transformation, or at least so we believe. Thus, to the problems that arise because we have mistaken the psychological mechanisms of person with the nature of person, we must add the problems that arise from the difference between the particulars of person and the usual kinds of data we get from the body. The former are different kinds of "data," and they require different kinds of thought for which physicians are simply not trained or prepared. But that deficiency, once recognized, should set our feet on new paths toward new goals.

In this chapter I have attempted to show that some of the disquiet people have over the failure of physicians to meet the human or personal needs of their patients arises from the failure of both physicians and society to realize that medicine is inherently a moral profession. Doctors make ethical decisions in concert with their patients all the time, but neither they nor the patients may be aware of this. Much of the equipment the physician brings to this task he develops through life experience rather than through specific training.

We have explored those factors in the history of medicine that, in artificially separating the person from the disease, have directed our awareness away from the nexus of the problem. Because of centuries of systematic neglect in medicine we find ourselves unable to even give a satisfactory definition of what we mean by "person." The great advances in psychiatry that at least brought an understanding of the emotional aspects of disease and finally returned the use of the word "psyche" to therapeutic honor still bypassed the nature of person.

In order to bring about the reunification of person and body in medicine, physicians will have to be trained or retrained to consider the essentially moral problems of the sick person as an important part of their professional concern. But it is not effective to tell physicians to be more moral or ethical; they do not consider themselves immoral or unethical. Rather, emphasis must be placed on sharpening the valuational thought processes required to make moral decisions just as we presently emphasize and sharpen the medical student's ability to think analytically in order to make scientific decisions. Valuational thought is not fuzzy thought; it is merely different from analytic thought. And the medical student must be taught to honor subjective information from patients as he presently honors objective data. The subjective is no less real or important in medicine, but simply a different kind of reality.

It is not sufficient or fair to force doctors to confront the necessity of accepting the responsibility of making moral decisions without offering training that will support the burden with expertise. The medical student learns not only what pneumonia is, but also how to treat it. Even as we recognize that each case of pneumonia is different, we know that medicine advanced because general principles could be laid down. It is fine to see courses in the humanities begin to enter medical education in an attempt to broaden the viewpoint of physicians, but that alone will never be sufficient. Something new must be added in medicine: a heightened consciousness of the human condition, citizenship for the subjective. Everyone knows that, in the uncharted fields of the systematic study of the moral and the nature of values, there is more quicksand than solid footing, but therein lies the challenge.

Why should such work take place in medicine? By their frequent references to physicians and to medicine,

Plato and Aristotle acknowledged that the care of the sick involves things central to the human condition. That same arena can still provide basic understanding. We are, in some sense, up against the edge of technology. We are not out of new technology, not by a long way, but we are fresh out of innocence. What is progress in medicine? The great cardiologist Samuel Levine once said that the intern of today was a better cardiologist than he himself had been after many years of practice. That is a good definition of progress. Is there any way of saying that the intern of tomorrow will be better at making moral decisions than the experienced practitioner of today? I see no evidence for that, although we desperately need progress in such aspects of medical care. And progress requires new directions.

A patient, her husband, and I sat talking for an hour or more in her hospital room before surgery for a mass in the breast. She was trying to decide what operation she would consent to should the lump turn out to be cancer. (She decided to allow the surgeon to do a modified radical mastectomy if it should be necessary, and it was.) It was clear that her decision had as much to do with her and her life as it did with what the pathologist would see under the microscope. There will always be painful scenes like this one in hospital rooms—the need for painful decisions whose difficulty arises because sickness occurs in persons.

To bring discipline to those decisions that involve persons as well as disease, to relieve that face of human suffering—that would be new, that would be a revolution in medicine. The search for such rigor is at the edge of a truly new frontier in medicine, where the moral and the technical, where person and body, come together.

4 The Healing Connection

A FIFTY-FOUR-YEAR-OLD MAN had varicose veins for years. Although they had become increasingly unsightly, he had accepted them as part of himself. His legs were not his best thing, he said to himself when he took his socks off at night. Then he developed a sore near his ankle that grew larger despite all the ointments, salves, and bandages he used. (The thought that his home remedies might only be making the sore worse frightened him. And besides, he remembered dimly from his childhood that his grandmother had a sore on her foot that had to be cut off.) His doctor told him that the sore was caused by his varicose veins and that he needed an operation on both legs to prevent the development of such sores. (How the doctor could be so sure after looking for just a moment at something that had plagued him for weeks really amazed him. If he hadn't known the doctor so well, he might not have trusted his opinion after such a quick look; instead, he took it as more evidence of what a good doctor he had.)

He had never been operated on before and was frightened at the prospect. He didn't know exactly what scared him, besides the general idea. His friends' comments (well meant, he was sure) made things worse by bringing up things he hadn't even known enough to worry about.

The surgeon was nice enough, and the hospital made a good impression on him. The operation was performed on a Monday, and the operation itself was not a bad experience, as he had had spinal anesthesia. On awakening in the recovery room, he had felt anxious because he couldn't feel or move his legs; but after the nurse told him that the effect of the anesthesia had not yet worn off, he felt comforted and fell asleep again. Even though his legs hurt after the operation, he felt a bit stupid about having been so frightened. On Thursday morning the surgeon told him that he could go home on Saturday, which was fine because he was beginning to get bored—and besides, he would be happy to have privacy again.

About 3 a.m. the next day he was nagged out of his sleep by some discomfort in the side of his chest that he decided must be gas. But he could not burp or pass gas and he could not find a comfortable position. He decided to call the nurse for some Alka-Seltzer or whatever they used in hospitals and searched his mind to remember what he had eaten the night before. While he waited for the nurse to come (it took as long as they all said), he began to get frightened and the pain became worse. He could not figure out what was so frightening because the pain wasn't that bad, although it was getting sharper and breathing made it worse. He thought briefly about his heart but dismissed that idea because the pain was on the wrong side. Then he thought that perhaps he had slept on his arm and that was why it hurt, though he could not remember that that had ever happened before.

When the nurse came, she listened to his story and

asked some questions. Looking at her face, he became more scared than before. She said something about getting the doctor and not to worry, but by that time he was so frightened that he hardly heard her.

Within minutes after she left the room, he was in agony. Every little breath or motion aggravated his condition. He then started to cough, which made the pain ten times worse. When he spat, there was blood on the Kleenex! Panic seized him briefly, but he was feeling so terrible and it was so hard to breathe that he could not organize his thoughts.

Soon there were doctors all around his bed. Although they had given him something for pain, he was sure that he would die—especially since no one told him anything, or if they did he did not understand it. No one seemed to want to let him sleep, although he was so tired he could have cried (or had he cried? he couldn't remember). He just wanted them to go away or to do something—or both.

The patient had a pulmonary embolus (clot in the lung) and after a week or so he made a complete recovery. His lungs are fine now, as are his legs. But neither he nor his wife will ever forget the event. How did he get well? Certainly the anticoagulants and other potent drugs for pain and sleep were important (although patients do recover without them). But many other things took place within him and around him that also played a part in his return to health. Those other factors in recovery, however, are so intrinsically a part of the scene, so automatic in the patient, the doctors, the nurses, and the family, that their role is all but invisible. It is those "invisible" elements in his becoming well that I should like to start examining in this chapter, for they are in the province of the physician as healer.

The great majority of the ill become whole again by themselves. But as no one is truly "by himself," getting well through "nature" alone must involve others in some indeterminate way.

Perhaps we should take a closer look at what being well involves. When you run you are not supposed to look at your feet; it gets in the way of running. When you drive you just look where you want to go and the car obeys. If you have to concentrate on how to drive, you are not a driver yet. So it is with all the functions of life: we just do without an awareness of doing. Life is function. Health, at least in part, incorporates the ability of the self to soar, allied with, but unhampered by and unaware of, the confines of the body—unaware at least consciously, for somewhere within there must be, in true health, a unity between self and body. The healthy have confidence in themselves and in their bodies, a confidence built on experience and fed by the sense of invulnerability.

Furthermore, we are always meeting someone else's needs and standards. From infancy we are urged to do and to be, although reluctance to grow seems always to be present. There is a desire to arrest at each stage—a reluctance to give up the known and comfortable. But another part within us pushes forward the individual creative urge that each has within. It is interesting that in this culture the words "aggressive" and "aggression" have a pejorative connotation and there is no good word to describe what is a universal healthy attribute. "Individuation" is what Jung called it, and its power for growth and health is called "ego strength" by psychoanalysts. Thus a combination of the push of individuation and the pull of society keeps us growing up and functioning. Each step forward involves a disconnection with the way we were and thus a loss of the self that was. Consequently, each step forward involves anxiety and the reawakening of the anxiety of the previous steps forward in growth. Anyone watching a child grow up sees that the trajectory is not smooth. There are stops and starts and sometimes even a slight falling backward. It is a common observation that if a child who has begun to talk gets sick or something bad happens, the child stops talking and it may be some time before attempts at real speech start again. However, growth has its way and, no matter how imperiled, continues on. The world around the child (parents and other adults) provides the guidance and helps reassure the safety of each step. Thus growth, health, and function involve a combination of an inner drive and an outer group demand. (Although, of course, in both person and group there are counteracting negative forces.) For our purposes it is important to remember not only the forward force but the fact that, with each gain, there is anxiety, along with the loss of the comfort associated with the previous established state.

The move from sickness to health is much like growth. The sick person, as stripped and helpless as an infant, has to be brought back. In our culture, when illness is sufficiently severe this is done by doctors. While their role as the curers of disease is well known to all of us, their role as healers remains obscure.

The world of illness is part of the reasoning process of the physician. He knows what is happening and what those happenings mean. He understands causes and through time has always "understood" them. Thus the first thing the physician provides is the reassurance that what is happening to the patient is not part of the unknown, not beyond control, but part of the rational world.

It is not that the patient himself has no knowledge or

theory. Everybody has some concept of anatomy and the working of the body parts, but the knowledge is certainly incomplete and maybe even incorrect. Incompleteness is the key problem because no conclusion about the meaning of symptoms can be reached that offers certainty. Thus, when someone has a symptom—an alien body sensation whose origin is not known to him—and he starts trying to figure out what it means, he uses the knowledge he has, but he finds that it is insufficient. Now he tries to bring to bear more information, perhaps another symptom from far afield or a memory of someone else's illness, but still no firm conclusion can be reached. You may be able, if you so decide, not to think about, say, the Pittsburgh Symphony, but it is virtually impossible not to think about your own unresolved symptoms. Fear inevitably begins to enter the calculations as the holes in the reasoning become more apparent.

One of my patients complained that sometime ago when she started having intermittent pains in her knees, she saw a doctor, who reassured her that the symptoms were unimportant. More recently she noted occasional swelling of her ankles and now she had pain in her back. When she called me about these symptoms, she said that she also had pain in her left kidney. On questioning her, I found that she had tied the symptoms together (wrongly) by ascribing the swelling and the pain to a retention of liquid because of a diseased kidney.

Thus the process continues, with the conclusions drawn from the incomplete knowledge often proving more frightening than the facts. While the person is healthy, the inadequacy of the knowledge causes no problems, but in illness huge gaps appear that themselves are a source of fear or that acquire secondary meaning. Furthermore, the patient has no cohesive system that can handle new information as it is presented by illness.

But the physician does have such an overall rational system. We know that it need not be correct, since for most of the history of medicine it has not been correct. In addition, the medicine man in other cultures is similarly able to help his patient with a system of thought that, in terms of modern physiology, may bear no relation to reality as we see it. But the reality that counts is cultural reality, and the system used by the healer or doctor need be accurate only in terms of the culture in which it is being used, for it serves to explain illness. The doctor's explanation connects the unknown and apparently uncontrolled phenomena the patient feels with the remainder of the patient's experience.

The importance of the doctor's explanation cannot be overemphasized. It is not merely his statement of what is wrong in diagnostic terms that is important but his explanation of the meaning of the diagnostic term. One might say that, when a physician speaks to a patient, the rules of grammar change. "You have a hiatus hernia" is a complete sentence in English, but not, if you will, in doctoring. To be complete for that purpose, the sentence must read, "You have a hiatus hernia, which means that a part of your stomach has been pushed up into the hole of the diaphragm through which the esophagus passes to join the stomach; and while this may cause you some discomfort, it is easy to take care of and will do you no harm." That "sentence" has three parts: what the trouble is (the diagnosis), what it means in body terms (the anatomic or physiological explanation), and what it means in person terms (what can be done about it and what will be the result). Readers may quickly see that a fourth term is miss-

ing from the "sentence"—the causal term, the "why" part
of the sentence, which for some patients is the most important because it helps fix the "blame" for the condition. I use the word "blame" because that is the sense in
which the cause is often sought, not only by the patient but
also by family, friends, and others in the group. Did the patient do it to himself? Did it come from overwork or strain
(as in "I've been under a lot of strain lately")? Is it heredi-
tary? All of these are acceptable reasons. But the one seemingly unacceptable causal term is fate. That something
should just happen out of the blue often seems the hardest
to accept because that gives evidence of how vulnerable all
of us are.

In situations in which fate, pure and simple, is the
operative agency, the healer in non-Western cultures has
an advantage over physicians. The healer is always able to
fix the blame on malignant spirits or an unappeased an-
cestor or a neighbor with the evil eye; in fact, this may be
one of his chief functions. We may be tempted to laugh
at such explanations but only because they are not culturally congenial. Actually, I have often wished for some
similar set of constructions to ease my own task.

In our society psychosomatic explanations of illness
have become extremely popular because they allow patients to fix the blame on the most comforting locus of
all—themselves. Why this is the most advantageous source
of blame lies at the heart of a feature of illness that is
most disturbing to the sick person: the loss of control that
occurs. If the person is the source of his own illness he
remains in control, even if it is a perverse kind of control.
"If I'm not so much in control of my body that I can keep
it well, at least I control it sufficiently so that it is I who
make it sick. It is not fate that has struck me, which would

indicate my loss of control, but I myself." We have rules in our culture against making ourselves sick, however. It is not considered proper to abuse one's own body to the point of illness. The beauty of psychosomatic explanations of illness lies in the fact that a person has made himself sick (remained in control), but it is not his fault; rather, it is the fault of his unconscious. And as we all "know," one cannot be held responsible for the acts of the unconscious—so much has this psychoanalytic concept become part of our culture.

The four parts of the medical sentence I have enumerated are always hanging in the air, so to speak. If the physician fails to fill in the missing information, the patient will obtain it elsewhere. It may be objected that if a person goes to a doctor with worrisome symptoms and the doctor (after appropriate examination) says that he has a "virus," the patient doesn't need all those other explanations. That is true, because he already knows the other answers. We are a medically sophisticated people and know, or think we know, a great deal about disease, so that we already have all those answers for many illnesses, especially the trivial.

Because the questions are always hanging in the air, the physician who does not take the initiative in providing the answers may become the unwitting ally of the patient's attempts to fix the blame somewhere, a "somewhere" that may be damaging. An example is the ready way that aging is used to explain symptoms. Patients often say, "I guess I'm just getting older, huh, and what can you expect when you get old but that things will happen?" When the doctor agrees, that helps confirm a patient's picture of aging as an inevitable process of contraction in which he is trapped, powerless to alter fate. On the basis of the physician's lightly spoken agreement with his belief as to where the blame is to be fixed, each new symptom is seen as more evidence of the inexorable decline to be associated with age. While aging is indeed a fact that cannot be denied, the power of individuals to control its effect on them and their lives also cannot be denied.

Throughout these discussions it is assumed that illness lies along the continuum of life and that what is learned in one illness serves to educate the patient about the body and illness in general. Therefore, almost any illness, no matter how trivial, becomes an opportunity for the doctor to educate his patient. It is commonly pointed out that the word "physician" is derived from the Greek, meaning "teacher." Indeed, in the Platonic dialogue *Phaedo* Socrates points out that the physician should teach his patients about medicine and the body. It is unfortunately rare to see that precept applied consciously in medical practice. But consciously or unconsciously the physician is *always* teaching his patients, and it would seem reasonable that he should give thought to what he teaches. In this era the underlying concept conveyed to patients seems to be that, if there is no technological answer to their problems (medication or surgery), there is no answer. There is little attempt to teach the extraordinary ability people have to make themselves well or the means by which they become the partner of medication or another therapeutic modality.

The point remains, however, that the physician's knowledge moves the world of illness from the unknown to the rational world.

More exciting (because we know less about it) is the manner in which the doctor's knowledge of disease provides a rational link between body sensation, thought, and the surrounding world that allows the patient to work on his illness. Doctors have trouble defining how patients "work on" their illnesses, but accept the conception in its broadest usage. They say, "He worked hard at getting better," or conversely, "He is not trying at all." They accept something called "the will to live," and all doctors know how serious it is when the sick person says, "I just don't care any more." Although they seem to accept the fact of the process, they do not understand it and are rarely able to use it consciously. Nevertheless, the physician operates in this realm.

In Lévi-Strauss's *Structural Anthropology*, he analyzes, in a chapter on the meaning of symbols, a Cuna Indian incantation used to facilitate difficult childbirth. Hour after hour the chant goes on, its individual verses constructed of a mixture of the religious symbols of the tribe and the process of childbirth. The good spirit embarks on a symbolic trip up the vagina and into the uterus, meeting and conquering first this bad spirit, then that. Step by step the obstructions that stand in the way of the child's passage through the birth canal are removed. Then the good spirit descends, repeating the removal of personified obstacles to birth. Important to us is the mixture of religious symbolism and anatomy—the provision of individual and rational meaning to anatomic structures. Equally important is the fact that the chant goes on for hours. The shaman is not merely providing a religious blessing but participating in the process of childbirth. Lévi-Strauss suggests that the shaman, by this long and detailed integration of the symbols of religion and the process of childbirth, is able to connect the rational thought processes of the mother to the physiological processes involved in childbirth. Thus equipped, the patient is able to actively aid in the birth.

As mentioned earlier, our preverbal body experience persists within all of us. Furthermore, there is reason to believe that many of our bodily responses are accessible to the preverbal sensorimotor intelligence. But the sensorimotor intelligence is not ordinarily accessible to rational voluntary use. The feats of yogis in controlling their bodies and the effects on the body that can be produced under hypnosis lead us to believe that the two things— the sensorimotor intelligence and voluntary action—can, under certain circumstances, be linked; that is, it is possible to bring some of the experience that exists in the sensorimotor intelligence to the service of volition, if not to the verbal or conscious reasoning portion of the mind. This can perhaps be seen most clearly in a hypnotic trance in which the subject can learn to control a specific portion of the body under the guidance of the operator. It is constantly amazing to see a hypnotized patient with asthma constrict or relax the bronchi at will (and produce or dissipate wheezing at the same time). Such phenomena are facilitated by teaching the patient the anatomy of the part of the body being controlled.

While trance-induced control of the body is difficult to conceive for those who have not watched it, similar control has become an everyday experience in one aspect of medicine—childbirth. The natural-childbirth methods combine education about the process of childbirth (so that the mother will know what to expect during labor and delivery) with exercises that teach breathing control and relaxation. In this rational world in which we live, one should perhaps pause before pointing out the similarity between natural childbirth and the healer's childbirth ceremony of the Cuna Indians. Nonetheless, the similarities are striking. In our culture we say that an educated patient is a better patient because she is able to participate in her own care. I am suggesting that an educated patient is one in whom conscious process has been connected to body process. Many physicians have had the experience of "talking" a patient through a difficult experience. It is often said that all the doctor did was to quiet the patient's fears, but what is left unsaid is how that helps make the body better. Recall here the story from the prologue of the patient with pulmonary edema in a Bellevue psychiatric ward in the middle of the night.

It is implied in the foregoing that connecting conscious process to body process is an active phenomenon. The physician does not merely say to the patient, as though he were writing a prescription, "If you think about how your chest is constructed and what is happening in there, things will get better." (For one thing, he would feel foolish saying it and, for another, it wouldn't work.) Instead, the physician helps make these connections by his "educating" function. But it is not merely his knowledge that serves the purpose. The doctor plays an active physical part in providing a link between symbolic reason and the body: he uses his hands.

To understand the role of the doctor's hands in healing, it is necessary to introduce the concept of the tenderness phenomenon. During the preverbal period of infancy, we have noted that communication between the infant and its inner and outer world takes place through physical sensations. An apparently discrete class of sensations is concerned with the interplay of tenderness between infant and mother (or mother surrogate). When the child experiences distress, the mother comforts it and the distress is eased. Comforting is done in various ways but involves light touch (caressing), deep touch (hugging or squeezing), motion (rocking), and/or sound (crooning), usually associated with warmth, taste, and smell. All these sensations communicate a special message of safety and security that is apparently essential to life. We know that institutionalized infants die of marasmus (progressive emaciation) if they do not receive these stimuli. Experiments have shown that the same need is present in infant monkeys. We know, in addition, that infants are able to read the body language transmitted to them. No matter what the mother intends to transmit in terms of love and security, if she is extremely tense and nervous the infant reacts with lack of ease or worse. I would guess that no person whose infancy has had tenderness will be entirely happy, safe, and secure unless he or she is receiving those messages or is giving them to another. Similarly, individuals in whose infancy the tenderness experience has been poor or aberrant may have special difficulties in later life either in accepting tenderness or giving it.

The importance of the tenderness phenomena can be seen in sex. Most discussions of sex, both professional and casual, are climax oriented. But when sex is limited to orgasm alone it is sterile; and masturbation is often regarded as a poor substitute for a partner, despite the evidence of Masters and Johnson that the masturbatory orgasm is at least as "good." The other components of sex that are generally unspoken (especially by men) are the tenderness phenomena of adult sex play. Their similarity to those directed toward infants will be obvious to most adults on a moment of reflection. Similarly apparent on reflection is the dissatisfaction or sense of incompleteness in the absence of tenderness, even if climax occurs. It is important to reiterate that although their importance and largeness in life are obvious when one thinks about them, the need and the phenomena are usually unspoken.

For tenderness phenomena to be received, the territorial defenses must be bridged. Territoriality in animals has received considerable attention in the last few years. Briefly stated, each animal seems to establish space around itself, intrusion into which by another animal arouses increasing aggression. The same phenomenon is seen in humans. Edward Hall, in his book *The Hidden Dimension,* relates territoriality to the use of living space by humans and refers to the communications involved as the "silent language." That is a term I would prefer to use for the whole group of communications of the sensori-motor intelligence. The tenderness phenomena are the antithesis of the territorial defenses. It is apparent that there could be no sexuality without passing through the territorial defenses, which I suspect is one of the functions of tenderness between adults. Tenderness, then, is a signal of safety and security and may evoke permission to pass the boundaries of personal territory. It seems to be needed by all of us and to be identifiable in other animal species as well. Why do we conceal from ourselves and others our great need for it? Perhaps it is because the need for tenderness is established at the time in the infant's life when the overwhelming fact is its utter helplessness. When we grow into adulthood, the fact of that helplessness must forever be concealed from awareness, and everything that reminds us of it must be driven underground.

The tenderness phenomena, however, are very important in the healer's function. Tenderness is associated with our parents, and we transfer our permissiveness in this regard to parent surrogates. The doctor stands as parent figure, and we transfer to him not only other aspects of the parental role, but also the right to lay hands on us, to be tender to us, and to pass through our territorial defenses.

I have been reluctant to use the word "transference" (just as I have tried to avoid using other words from the psychoanalytic tradition in order to avoid an instant reaction, positive or negative, to the word that might obscure the content), but it seems necessary to deal with it, if only briefly.

As we are all aware, the analysis of transference plays an important part in psychoanalysis. The reaction of the patient to the therapist contains within it a replay of the reaction to the parent. Because of this, transference has received considerable attention in psychiatric literature and in literature on the doctor-patient relationship. Yet we know little about what transference really is. It seems to have physical as well as emotional meanings, since it is virtually impossible to make a distinction between emotional and physical feelings. A feeling is, by definition, a body sensation as well as a thought. Except abnormally, the two cannot be distinct: when one feels angry, there are body sensations. So too with feelings of happiness, joy, confidence, and love.

Transference is, I believe, a specialized usage of a normal bonding phenomenon, necessary to the individual for completeness or wholeness. Freud's early discussions of transference focused heavily on its object-directed sexual nature and thus set the tone for much of the extensive literature devoted to it, obscuring the essential normalcy of the underlying phenomenon. In the same manner, sexual feeling is part of total normal feeling and is to be distinguished from the sexual feelings directed at a specific person. Because of the frequent necessity for repressing the person-directed sexuality in normal growth and development, the component of normal feeling tone that is sexual is also repressed. We use the word "transference," but could just as well speak of connectedness, as long as we are aware that the connectedness involves the whole range of points of contact between two people from thought to feeling.

Important to our consideration of the topic is that the bonding, connectedness, or transference of the sick to the healer is not unidirectional. Both the doctor and the sick person become exquisitely sensitive to each other. Thus the sick person is as able to sense anxiety on the part of the doctor as the doctor is on the part of the patient. Indeed, that openness of the flow of feeling back and forth enables the physician to use his own feeling in the presence of the patient for therapeutic purposes. What is required is that the physician be prepared to accept the fact that a feeling within him can come from the patient. Experience is required because we are used to assuming that, if we have a feeling, it comes from within ourselves and we set about explaining or rationalizing the feeling to ourselves. In the bonding phenomena between the doctor and the sick, the feeling the doctor has may have originated in the sick person. I remember working at the bedside of a man who for a long time had been ill from a variety of serious diseases. The management of the various problems—kidney, heart, diabetes—was difficult but challenging until the day I had the feeling of hopelessness at that bedside. When I returned the next day, I again felt hopeless and was disturbed at myself for feeling that way, since I rarely do so. It suddenly occurred to me that the feeling of hopelessness might be coming from the patient. A few moments of conversation proved that to be true. After reassuring the patient, I was able to proceed with the management of the problems.

Another important aspect of the transference phenomenon seems to be that the sicker the patient, the more access the physician has to the core of the mind-body interface. That has a mystical sound only because we are not accustomed to the concept that it is possible to speak directly to the body and have it obey! Within limits, however, that appears to be true. Remember the patient with pulmonary edema on the psychiatric ward I mentioned in the prologue. There it was my desperation that caused me to start talking to her body through her. It was also my desperation that kept me from being embarrassed at the foolishness of the words. It does, in the beginning, make one feel foolish to speak that way to a patient, especially since the form of the language is direct and unambiguous and one rarely speaks that way normally. But this technique is applicable only to the frightfully sick, whose responses seem to approximate those of hypnotized people in the trance state.

The bonding phenomenon, then, is just part of the way in which the physician uses his knowledge to "connect" the patient's symbolic reasoning to his body. In addition, as we have seen, he may use his hands to reinforce the connection. Finally, he can comfort and reassure in a manner so basic that it is related to experiences in early infancy. His ability to make these connections with the patient does not stand apart from his other acts as a healer but is woven into the entire fabric of the healing function.

5 Omnipotence Regenerated

FEELINGS OF OMNIPOTENCE and omniscience are so often a striking aspect of the personality of individual physicians as to be practically a hallmark of the profession. Laymen often characterize doctors as arrogant. Doctors' attitudes toward their own illnesses are frequently marked by such foolish feelings of indestructibility and denial as to be simply incredible.

Many of the situations faced by a physician in the care of patients are sufficiently different from what he has been taught that his decisions are often based on little sure knowledge. Furthermore, the decisions he does make are frequently based on probabilities, sometimes including the possibility of awful consequences. The result is that doubt is the doctor's constant companion, doubts and fears that, except for rare circumstances, cannot be shared with his patient. As time goes on he seems surer and surer of himself, but the sureness is not always justified.

I have in mind two physicians who seem so sure of themselves that it is difficult to conceive of doubt ever entering their minds. The firmness of their words, the decisiveness of their actions, seem to leave little room for doubt. But I have worked with both of them when things weren't going so well, when fear of error filled the night. Alas, they, like me, were nagged by doubt.

"When am I going to be like that?" said one of the medical students I was teaching at that time. "Like what?" "Like Dr. X. You know . . . so sure of myself." I think I was honest enough to say that like Dr. X, the student would probably learn to appear sure of himself; but if he were really good, he would never be sure of himself.

Obviously, in the course of practicing medicine, some decisions that were difficult to make in the beginning become easy, even second nature, but new situations are always arising and the well of doubt never seems to run dry. In caring for patients, the doctor must learn to deal with, and conceal, the doubts and fears by some mechanism or another. The sick patient has enough troubles and he doesn't need his doctor's doubts. The essential fact of medicine is that decisions must be made if for no other reason that no decision is in itself a decision. As an Army doctor, I worked with a surgeon so beset by doubt that he couldn't bring himself to operate. At ten o'clock at night a patient would come in with obvious appendicitis. We would discuss the case hour after hour through the night, and finally, at five o'clock in the morning, with everybody exhausted, the surgeon's confidence was sufficiently bolstered so that the surgery could proceed.

The image of omnipotence is an essential component of the healer. And his badge of invincibility apparently grows. I remember an apt description of a doctor in a novel that said: "Although he was small and physically unimposing, he spoke like someone who was used to having people do what he told them." So the doctor's life experience strengthens his already strong sense of omnipotence. His patient needs it. We saw how illness puts cracks in the essential shield of omnipotence all of us have and how damaging it is to lose the sense of omnipotence, how insecure we are when our frailty becomes known to us—who will put Humpty Dumpty together again? The doctor's feeling of omnipotence is thus essential to his role. His posture of omnipotence may annoy the healthy and infuriate the nurses—but how important it is for the sick. The patient borrows it, clothes his nakedness in it until such time as his own becomes whole again—as it does during the process of recovery from illness.

It is interesting that perhaps the seemingly most omnipotent of all physicians are the neurosurgeons, and theirs is the specialty in which nature's odds are most against them. In terms of curing, they are the least effective. In addition, they operate on the brain, the most mysterious part of the body. Does any diagnosis strike such terror as brain tumor? The brain surgeon's incredible feeling of omnipotence helps protect us from our fear.

The same sense of omnipotence that protects the patient endangers the doctor because he is rarely aware of it or its place in medical care. Omnipotence is magical power; it defies the realities of life. As time goes on, the distinctions between magic and reality become hazy and the magic is reinforced—reflected in his patient's eyes. Error may become, in the doctor's mind, less possible, and he stands the danger of functioning primarily with magic rather than with knowledge. He heals—puts together—but may begin to fail in curing as his knowledge lags. Once he begins to believe that he, rather than his knowledge and technical skill, is the source of the cure, danger lurks in the image reflected back from his patient's eyes. If the doctor looks into those eyes, the image that he sees is— God. But that image is the enemy.

For the same reason physicians are denied much of the satisfaction and pleasure laymen think they must be getting from their work. Just as they must learn not to blame themselves for every death or failure of medicine, knowing that nature and disease are powerful enemies, so must they learn not to take the credit for every success. Nature is also a powerful ally. Most patients would have gotten better anyway, or any other doctor could have made them better. Self-satisfaction takes the edge off skill and lowers the doctor's guard. The unwary physician is soon in trouble, as error always waits for the unguarded moment.

The profession of medicine, as part of its own culture, has built some safeguards against the abuse of the sense of omnipotence. I know of no other structured area of human activity in which open self-criticism is so much a part. From the earliest days in medical school the doctor is taught to admit his own errors openly among his peers. Conferences at a teaching hospital are devoted to examining each operation or every death to see if proper care was given. When laymen chance to attend these conferences, they are often amazed at the amount of peer criticism tolerated by an individual physician. Especially in large hospitals someone is always looking over the doctor's shoulder. Like members of a religious order, the individual doctors concede the greater degree of omnipotence to the profession. The institution is ceded greater invulnerability than its practitioners. The hospital may also be granted by the patient the same, or even a greater, degree of omnipotence. Thus, patients who greatly admire a particular hospital may readily give themselves over to the care of unknown doctors assigned by the institution, since those physicians are cloaked in the magic of their hospital.

Just as the doctor's sense of omnipotence is used by both the doctor and the patient to shield the patient from the nakedness of his frailty, so too is the physician's connectedness a powerful tool in healing. The doctor is connected in several ways. He is a solid, trusted member of society with high status so that he is firmly rooted in the real world of the healthy. Moreover, along with the clergy he is given the right to walk in the very different world of the sick and the dying, a world that threatens the well, who must defend themselves against its existence—even the doctor himself is threatened with the knowledge of its peril. Because the doctor can journey through both worlds with seeming impunity, he is the bridge between the worlds of life and death. The clergyman offers a comforting exit, but the doctor offers a chance to return. The patient, withdrawn deeper and deeper into himself as his sickness worsens, is protected from falling off the world by the reassuring hand of his doctor. As noted earlier, certain symptoms, such as the sensory disturbances (loss of vision, hearing difficulties, dizziness), in themselves cause disconnectedness and the doctor's knowledge helps contain the limits of the fear they engender. But to see connectedness only in these narrow senses is to miss its importance in illness and healing.

Similarly, the sick person's loss of control over his world is eased by the healer. He becomes the patient's agent ("he's *my* doctor"), and his control over the environment becomes the patient's control.

In certain very manipulative patients the control is more direct, since they control, or attempt to control, the doctor. The extent of their success is often amazing, as the doctor finds himself doing things to and for the patient that he would not ordinarily consider doing. Such attempts at control may extend to the patient's family. One patient whose cancer had spread beyond the ability of his physician to help was the husband of an extremely demanding and manipulative wife. The wife asked permission to use Krebiozen, a drug thought then and subsequently shown to be a fake. Initially none of the attending doctors wanted anything to do with it, but the wife, arguing the futility of other treatment, persuaded them to approve. The drug arrived with the fanfare of the Hope diamond, and the wife carefully read the instructions that were addressed to *her*. It must be administered by a doctor and given just so, she said. Would one of the doctors on her husband's case please give it? Before long, and carefully observing the nonsensical and magical precautions accompanying its use, one of the physicians who had opposed the whole business found himself giving the injections. The patient was helpless in his disease and was represented by his wife (equally denied her usual activity by the husband's illness), who pressured the doctor into doing something that was completely objectionable to him. The patient died shortly thereafter, and the wife angrily blamed the death on the "fact" that X rays taken of her husband interfered with the action of the Krebiozen. Her anger should have been anticipated by the physicians, because they had abdicated their healing role.

Similarly, in the current demands for community control of hospitals and medical care, other factors latent to the problem are involved, just as most of healing as a function is latent in medical care. When and if the "community" acquires the control, the institutions and doctors will be surprised to find the "community" even more angry with them. The community, in demanding control, may be pointing out the failure of the physicians and the hospitals to meet their responsibility as healers. I do not believe that control is what is desired as much as a return of the professional to his more complete role as curer *and* healer. On the other hand, healing places a very heavy personal demand and responsibility on the healer, and we are not surprised to find the younger physician abrogating that responsibility as he finds the "true" importance of his profession in other jobs, such as politics.

The physician is set apart by his function and, as much as he doesn't want to be "hierarchical" or "elitist," he is seen by others in this role. When he tries to reach out to others as though he were simply himself, an ordinary person, he may be crossing boundaries of which he was unaware and may do damage or cause hurts that were not his intention. The mistake is to confuse himself, the man, with himself, the physician. As a man he is indeed no different than others, but as a doctor he is a representative of the body in its war against fate, sickness, and death. The boundaries of that role cannot be made to go away because an individual physician wants them to or because ideology suggests that there are no boundaries.

Not only does sickness cause the patient to lose control of the environment but, even more fundamentally, it causes him to lose control of his body. We noted previously that health is the ability of the person to soar above the body, allied with but unhampered by its confines. In health the body responds to every reasonable command. How different is illness, when the ailing part, no matter how strongly commanded, refuses to do as it is asked. But more, the balance between self and body has been altered. The body has become a dangerous, alien thing. Take, for example, the person who has been told that his slightly swollen leg has thrombophlebitis—clots in the veins—and that he needs treatment to prevent a clot from breaking off and going to the lungs. The patient may then view the leg, not much cause of distress in itself, as though it were a loaded shotgun pointed at his head, cocked and ready to go off. Or the person who, having once bled badly from an ulcer, for months thereafter sees in any symptom the sign of the return of the bleeding. His fear may be aroused not so much by the illness itself but by the memory of how poorly controlled his body was during the episode.

Similarly endangered is the woman whose cancer has been treated into remission. Each visit to the doctor becomes a nightmare of anticipation. Will the tests show the cancer to be starting up again? The patient has lost faith in her ability to read her body. The original disease was discovered when she felt well; and now no body sensation, pleasant or unpleasant, seems to be a trustworthy guide. If the tests are normal, joy abounds, but perhaps only briefly, to be followed by depression—anger at being thus trapped —because even in the good news lie the seeds of the bad. Possibly the tests were wrong. Maybe the doctor made a mistake; maybe he is lying (he didn't seem as cheerful as usual). The patient is like a fish on a hook; even when the line is not pulled taut, the fish knows that the hook is there.

A final example is the patient who had polio in childhood and who struggled through the long, arduous process of rehabilitation, a history of pain and orthopedic operations marking her gains. She has finally achieved a tenuous mastery of her body, often bought at a high price, that enables her to get on with her life. Much of the memory of it all has been repressed, but the memory remains, nevertheless, always ready to be reactivated. A day of sight-seeing at the same pace as others is followed by painful muscles and aching joints. Pain like that means trouble, disability—a loss of the thin hold on life. For the other sightseers the same tired and aching muscles are taken lightly; but then their past is different, and they have confidence in their bodies.

Each example is different, but each is similar in that the relation of person to body has been sufficiently altered that each person is trapped by the body, has lost control, and is fearful. In each the actual state of the body is not the problem. The disability is not body disability but rather fear of the body—fear of the future compounded in many by memory of the past disability, but, above all, fear. In each instance cited, the fear has a basis in reality. Pulmonary emboli—clots in the lung—are life-threatening. Gastrointestinal bleeding is serious. The return of the cancer may signal the beginning of suffering and the end of life. The return of crippling for the polio patient may mean the end of an active life. But in each instance, at the moment the patient seeks help from the doctor, the enemy is not the body; the enemy is fear. The body is out of the control of the self.

In each case the actual treatment that might be offered by a physician is not a matter of much dispute or wide alternative. The attitude of the physician, what he perceives to be his goal, what he wants the patient to learn —these are crucial to what will happen to the patient in each of these situations. Here the healing function can be seen as clearly distinct from the curing function; and while the technological alternatives are narrow, the possible differences in attitude and goal are huge.

Even the kind of humane physician who sees his job as limited to the cure of disease has something to offer only the first patient, the man with the thrombophlebitis. The others have no disease. To all he can offer reassurance, but of what value is the reassurance except to the first patient? To the patient who had previously bled from ulcers, reassurance cannot remove the memory of his loss of control and poor performance during the previous bleeding. Reassurance to the woman in remission from cancer does not remove the sword hanging over her (especially in this day when everybody is so medically sophisticated), and reassurance might calm the woman who once had polio but cannot change her dire interpretation of the episode of sore muscles, the reminder of her limitation. In this day of cancer, chronic disease, and the problems of the aging, patients typified by the last three cases far out-number those like the man with clots in his veins. There has to be, and there is, something more to give than reassurance, something more to teach than patience, and some greater goal than acceptance. The most important thing the physician has to offer and teach all but the first patient is control of the body.

What does control of the body mean? It would be best to acknowledge from the start that I am going to have trouble clarifying the meaning. The difficulty arises from several sources. First, the concept is essentially nonverbal, and it is difficult to use words to express what is a feeling or a state of mind. Second, the concept of control of the body is not culturally congenial. We are devoted to the mind, not to the body (although this attitude seems to be changing somewhat). But current back-to-the-body tendencies, such as touch or sensitivity training, have acquired a certain quality of instant joy (perhaps undeserved), which is inappropriate to the sick. Third, what I am discussing occurs through time, and it is the process, not the finished product, that is vitally important to the ill. Since the control of which I am speaking is a part of growth, there is no finished product, just as it would be difficult to know when a person is a finished product. Finally, we are back to the mind-body problem that has troubled us for many centuries.

Perhaps the way to proceed is that which has always served physicians best: to return to the clinical problem. The prototypical patient is the one who had polio in childhood and who identifies her body with its restrictions and feels anger at those restrictions. Because of that, if the doctor explains to her that the muscle aches and joint pains are of no permanent significance, he will be believed on only a superficial level; her memory of the past blocks deeper acceptance. If, after careful examination, the doctor says that there is no evidence of structural damage and that the pains and aches are therefore not indicative of decreased capacity, but are instead evidence of unused but potentially useful *increased* capacity and *lessened* disability, the statement may be met by frank disbelief. After all, the doctor says, one can't have muscle pain without having muscle. With training the muscle and joints can (within limits) be made stronger and more limber, endurance increased, and function improved. The physician goes on, saying that he can show her how to accomplish this goal and how to have more control over the body. "That will be the day," she replies, generally ending the conversation. The problem is not that she wouldn't like all those things to happen or even that they are viewed as impossible, but that they call to mind the original rehabilitation and its unpleasantness. Moreover, she simply doesn't have any idea of what controlling the body means: she doesn't control her body; her body controls her.

Each of us strikes some balance with his body. It can be loved, neglected, disdained, admired, denied, but it cannot be ignored. It cannot be ignored because it continually makes demands for food, warmth, sleep, and so on, demands that simply must be met if we are to function effectively. There is a certain automatic quality in the demands and in the way they are generally met. We do not consider food, sleep, or warmth a demand of the body; we simply think that we are hungry, tired, or cold and do something about it. The automatic aspect comes about because we have organized our lives in a manner that almost makes the body, as a demanding agent, invisible. Let the circumstances of the world change and the demand becomes a controlling monster. One of my friends described how during the famous Battle of the Bulge in December of 1944 (in which he was eventually wounded) all he ever thought about was where he was going to move his bowels next (a dilemma recognizable by anyone who has chronic diarrhea and lives in normal surroundings). Similarly, we can read about the horror of the Andes survivors and their cannibalism as a story of people completely at the mercy of their bodies.

The world we live in, then, is set up in a way that allows automatic responses to bodily needs and the body's architecture. To the disabled living in the same world, automaticity may be a luxury denied them: the height of steps, the lowness of a chair, a three-block walk, a typewriter, all require special effort and may serve as constant reminders of the limitations of the body. In such cases the person is generally passive, and if he does express resentment at his limitations we generally counsel passivity: we say he must learn to accept his limitations. Thus the anger at the body seems natural in the face of the constant reminders of its limitations and of the need to accept them. A few moments' reflection will show that a disabled person and a "normal" person differ only quantitatively. Everyone is limited by his body, and those limits increase with age. Moreover, few people are satisfied with their bodies. This attitude is prevalent among women to whom an ideal of beauty is always being held up, but it is also true of men. One may argue with the characterization of the attitude toward the body as passive. After all, women and men are forever going on diets and starting exercise programs, and considering the violent way these projects are attacked, one can hardly use the word "passive." In a way, the final effect of most of these regimens is to reemphasize the lack of control the person has over his body. The weight loss is followed by weight gain and the exercise program is soon stopped. The lesson that is learned is the futility of the struggle.

Actually, since the feeling of helplessness is always so uncomfortable, the control that is exercised is the control of the failure. ("I'm always going on diets.") It is also true that after repeated failures (often starting in adolescence), the excess weight has acquired meanings far removed from the weight itself and having little to do with the actual physical problem (interaction with parents or spouse, for example). The problems are confounded by the time allotted to weight loss, figure control, and so on. The twenty-one-day course of figure exercises, the ten-day diet, the three-week beauty program are typical. What someone wants is to move from the state of being fat to the state of slimness or from the state of flabbiness to the state of trimness. The process of getting there (prudent eating or exercise) is of no interest or may even be unpleasant.

There is a limit to how long anyone will put up with that which is painful or boring, or a deprivation. Unfortunately, while three weeks may be the limit of one's ability to remain in self-induced pain, the body does not change that way. I do not mean that weight won't come off in three weeks. When it does, however, it goes right back on, because only the secondary problem was attacked. The primary problem is not weight but eating habits, and it takes many, many months to permanently affect a life-style problem such as eating habits. Furthermore, no one continues to endure a constant source of pain such as being deprived of everything "good" to eat. Such change has to come about very gradually, and the reward has to be the change itself, since weight loss will be real but very slow. Unfortunately for the physician who tries to teach the control of the body, such unrealistic time goals, because they are all around us, make it difficult to maintain realistic objectives.

It is obvious that as children we had to learn to control our bodies in order to grow up. Although such mastery is often long in coming and hard won, it, too, is automatic. Body mastery, like speech, is not a matter of choice for the child; it just happens—for some better than others, for some faster than others, but for all to a degree sufficient to live automatically in our world. Here, as in all other aspects of growth and development, parental influence helps determine the relationship that the emerging adult will have to the body. When the mother shares her great fears of illness or the sense that her children are fragile, it is not surprising to find the adult similarly fearful of the body. When Oedipal conflicts (such as the fear of winning) are re-created in sports, attitudes toward body control are again partially determined. And, of course, many of the early psychological traumas of childhood are *physical* (there is no mind-body distinction in infancy) and carry over into adulthood as physical fears and hypochondriasis.

Cultural conventions also play their part. Recent increasing acceptance of women athletes and athletics for women serves to point up previous and still strong attitudes that a woman's body is more for attraction and display than for use. It is my belief that at least part of the anger against male doctors displayed in the women's movement is really anger at their own bodies for being (in their culturally determined eyes) inferior to men's, with the male doctor being the symbol of the body. (Another large part of this anger seems justified by the male chauvinist behavior of doctors.) For women, then, command of the body may be an even more remote concept than for men.

All these things from cultural attitudes to infantile trauma contribute to closing the patient's mind to the concept of control of the body and to preventing him or her from seeing the unity of mind and body as a most desirable and attainable state.

The greatest problem presented to us by the automatic growth of body mastery in childhood is that it leads to the belief that in aging decline in body mastery is also automatic. It is not at all clear, however, that the changes that occur with aging inevitably lead to disability and decline until very late in old age. Growth is obligate in childhood and decline is obligate in *far* advanced age, but functioning in the intervening years is under far more voluntary control than is generally considered. Here, too, it is difficult to convince someone who is older that creaking joints may not be a signal to cut back but rather an imperative to rehabilitate them by increased activity. Unfortunately, as noted previously, the physician who attributes symptoms to old age without providing a solution is really telling the patient to cut back, to give way in the face of the inevitable. The years are inevitable, but the disability may not be. The rule seems to be that if you want to be active late into the seventies and eighties, be active early in the seventies whether the activity is running, fencing, or sex.

If I could banish one word from medicine, it would be the word "arthritis." The patient has pain in the neck or the back or pain arising from a "pinched nerve." X rays show the calcium deposits characteristic of age, and the patient is told that he has arthritis. With that word the doctor pronounces the inevitable decline of aging, which the patient has to accept. Although there are inevitable changes in the body that occur with aging, what concerns us is not structural change, such as the deposit of calcium (which may be, technically, arthritis), but how we function. Life is function. It is a gross error to confuse the bony structure of the back with its functioning. The back is a complex of bones, cartilage, tendons, and muscles that function as a unit. To be healthy it needs strength, flexibility, and suppleness, and these characteristics involve all the parts of the back. They can often be restored to excellent function in people whose X rays show advanced "arthritic changes." Backs are not merely bones, any more than people are only a collection of organs. The word "arthritis" can be more disabling than the body state it represents.

For these reasons, teaching the patient to understand and control the body would seem essential. If pain and sickness are great enough and if there are no easy technological alternatives, the patient may be receptive. After all, if a simple medication will solve the problem it would be foolish to do it the hard way. But (and this is the usual situation) if illness has gone on for years or is severe enough and the outlook is dire, most people will try anything.

A fifty-year-old woman had recurrent abdominal pain for ten years. Several operations had not helped and had left other symptoms in their wake. The cause of the pain was not at all clear, and increasingly she was told that "it was all in her mind." She was referred to me by the surgeon who, although he felt that the pain was not emotional in origin, could find no cause and believed that he had nothing more to offer her. Her life had become organized around the attacks of pain that would occur frequently and would sometimes disable her for days, since they would usually be accompanied by nausea, then vomiting and diarrhea. Because eating would aggravate the pain, her diet had become bizarre. She used inordinately large amounts of tranquilizers and pain relievers, which, in themselves, added to her problems. Characteristically, early in the attack she would try to avoid "giving in to it" and her activity would worsen the episode.

I, too, believed by its pattern and other characteristics that her illness was organic, although it was clear to me that many emotional symptoms had become attached to her pain. She walked, talked, and moved as though to convince others that she was sick. She had, in the past, vigorously defended herself against even the suggestion of psychiatric help, which she saw as an attempt to prove that her illness was "psychological." She distrusted all doctors categorically (except the surgeon who had referred her)—a characteristic of almost anyone whose illness has gone on long enough, especially if pain is involved.

I tried to teach her ways of controlling her pain and other symptoms: how to use diet, how to combine medications for their greatest efficacy with fewest side effects, how to pace herself, when to rest and when to be active, in order to gain the greatest amount of pain-free functional time. I got virtually nowhere. Months passed. Visit after visit was devoted to her telling me why everything I suggested wouldn't work. (Everybody will recognize "Yes, but" behavior.) I became increasingly exasperated and couldn't understand how I had gone so wrong. I even found myself saying, "You'd think you wanted to keep your pain," for which there was much evidence but no reason to say it. Nonetheless, the patient's trust increased and I felt it unfair to betray the trust by quitting.

In January she was admitted to the hospital for what had become a yearly ritual attempt to find some cause for the pain by repeating all the tests and X rays. I knew that I was seeing the problem wrongly and then, just before visiting her on my rounds one day, the solution occurred to me. I asked her how she felt and she was as noncommittal as usual. When I became visibly annoyed, she said that she would have felt better had it not been for the nurse the night before who told her that it was all in her mind. She went on a while and then said that she didn't care about that nurse. That wasn't true, I said: she *did* care. As a matter of fact, that nurse controlled her. Anybody who told her that the pain was in her mind controlled her. Moreover, any food, any act, anything that made the pain worse controlled her. Then I reiterated the goals we had been trying to accomplish for months and suggested how much better she would be if she used them to regain control of her life.

On that basis we started over again, more successfully. The gains were slow but real. With increasing control of her pain, her face, her clothing, her walk, her whole attitude changed. The concept of control of the body—of riding the body, no matter how damaged it might be, instead of being ridden by it—had finally penetrated. There are still many problems to be solved, but the basis for the solutions is now there.

It is common to see patients with chronic disease acting as if they wanted to keep the disease rather than be rid of it. Considering some of the suffering involved, the idea seems ridiculous unless one understands the need each of us has to control his universe. Sickness robs us of that control. What are the alternatives in recurrent illness? The patient can wait out each episode, helpless, frightened, and usually increasingly depressed. The patient can struggle against the symptoms (such as shortness of breath in asthma), but that only makes them worse. The body cannot be forced to be well; that approach simply doesn't work. Nonetheless, one sees sick people doing just that year after year: struggling against a symptom despite the fact that they know the futility of such behavior from bitter experience. But at least in the struggle they are asserting themselves, maintaining their identity by refusing to "give in." The physician may be enlisted to participate in their struggle, so that long after he has run out of rational therapies he finds himself giving medications or treatments that he knows are valueless, or worse.

If the episodic illness is not too severe the person may disregard it, getting on with his life and carrying a burden of symptoms that would send most of us to emergency rooms. But such people learn to tolerate the pain or difficulty to an amazing degree. Often one finds them neither taking medications nor doing the simple things that would ease their distress, as though to do so would threaten the uneasy peace with their disease that has been established. Such an attitude may be extremely effective, except that it does nothing to lessen the cumulative toll of the illness and prepares them poorly for the time, should it come, when the disease worsens. Often the other face of denial is panic.

There is still another alternative. The person may find that, when he is sick, his family becomes more attentive, his world more amenable to manipulation. It doesn't take too many episodes of illness (asthma is a good example because it can be very frightening to the onlooker and it is virtually impossible to have a severe attack unknown to others) before the person realizes what a potent instrument the illness is for controlling his private domain. Then the physician may begin to find that nothing he tries is successful in controlling the symptoms; and, as he explores further, he suspects that his patient doesn't want to get well. Indeed, as in the example cited earlier, such patients will not get well until they are given an alternative method of control.

It might be well to emphasize that simply telling the

patient what he is doing is useless, or worse. On the most superficial level, the explanation has no point unless the doctor is prepared to offer an alternative solution and to prove its effectiveness. In addition, the patient's behavior will seem so irrational to himself (he does not produce his sickness consciously) that he may not believe what the doctor has told him, and the doctor may then become an enemy in his fight for survival.

Moreover, the psychological and physical mechanisms involved are so complex that the doctor runs the risk of oversimplifying his explanation, thus allowing the patient to think that the doctor simply does not understand. And in long-standing illness the situation does get complicated, as in the following case.

A patient has had asthma since the age of four, which has come and gone throughout her life. Now, in her twenties, the patient sees asthma not as a disease but as a part of her, like her leg or her personality. She is so allergic to dogs that she may start wheezing during a discussion about them (leading others to think that her asthma is emotional or that she is "putting it on" when, in fact, a conditioned reflex has developed over the years). An emotionally charged discussion may provoke asthma as it recalls other situations where asthma occurred. Her wheezing may complicate a common cold, and the patient may react with anger at herself for wheezing and hence not take her medications, making the attack worse. To the bystander the act of not taking medicine seems to be deliberately and intentionally worsening the attack when, in reality, she is getting even with her body. Or the asthma may be directly related to some unconscious conflict. It is a brave physician who tries to teach such a patient to control her asthma by oversimplified reassurance. The relationship of mind and body is hardly understood, and the word "psychosomatic" stands for a concept but rarely for a known mechanism or real understanding.

Finally, when an authority such as the doctor says that the patient doesn't want to get better or is producing his own illness, in an odd way that person legitimates the patient's behavior. The very words, in the absence of alternative solutions, indicate that such behavior is possible, even common. Similarly, many interpretations by psychotherapists (not insights truly arising within the patient, which have a salutary effect), instead of becoming reasons for giving up some life pattern, become rules for behavior.

Teaching such patients how to control their bodies is a difficult task, and sometimes an impossible one. The sick person must be motivated. In Chapter 1, I described a man with angina pectoris sufficiently severe to prevent him from walking three blocks. When the extent and progressive nature of his disease became clear, he knew that he could no longer ignore it. That was in the early days of coronary-artery surgery and the prospect of an operation was to him, to say the least, less than pleasant. When exercise as therapy was offered he was extremely motivated, despite the fact that little was known about it then and he would be doing something considered crazy by friends and relatives. As the months went by and his angina became progressively less frequent, he not only felt better but had also learned something about himself and his body. He was able to stick to the exercise and to make himself better.

It is not my intention to engage in the controversy about exercise and the heart (although my own belief must be evident), but the benefit to the patients always includes a change in their view of themselves vis-à-vis their body. They have made themselves better. Sometimes the patient can be coaxed into the approach merely by being taught more effective ways of using medication. In this approach medication is not simply something given by a physician, with the patient following his instructions; instead, the patient learns what the drugs do and how they do it, and the drugs become things the patient manipulates—evidence of the patient's control of the disease, rather than of his dependence on the physician and his subjugation to the disease. Disdain of medication and pills is a luxury of health. For someone who has lived in fear of a bad attack of asthma, learning how to give oneself an injection of adrenalin—even if it is never needed—can mean freedom from fear. Fear is an enemy quieted much more effectively by control than by simple reassurance. The healthy simply do not comprehend the sick person's fear of a chronic symptom. Pain does not get easier to tolerate the longer it recurs; rather, it becomes more difficult, in part because the fear of its return compounds the discomfort. The body braces against its return, only making things worse. And so it is with vomiting, diarrhea, weakness, fatigue, and so on, through the list of troubles to which the body is host. Fear is the enemy.

Exercise of some kind frequently plays a large part in learning to control the body, not only because of its direct benefits but because it shows how tractable the body is. If only one steadily *leans* against the body's limitations, those limits gradually expand. Furthermore, it proves that one can do it, can get out there each time and do what is necessary. Finally, it teaches the importance of realistic time goals in body change. Given enough time, the body does change and the change is cumulative.

In all of this the physician is the teacher. While many healthy people learn these lessons by themselves, the sick need help. The attitude of regarding the body as an object of fear cannot be altered simply by telling someone not to be afraid. And such a change does not happen overnight. Each time some problem comes up, the patient is taught what it means and how to deal with it. The teaching takes time, but often, considering the alternatives, much time is saved.

While I frequently find hypnosis to be a very useful technique in caring for the sick, I do not use it primarily for what it allows me to do for the patient but rather as a means of teaching the patient to use his own capacity to control or retrain his body. I hesitate to discuss the use of hypnosis because people tend to be too fascinated with the phenomenon itself and too distracted by their misconceptions (which are legion) and thus miss the basic point.

One of the central features of illness is the loss of control. The doctor's job is to return control to his patient. Any method used to implement that goal may be useful. But whatever techniques are used in these situations are not an end in themselves; they are simply another means.

The doctor's sense of omnipotence is an important part of his function as a healer, something he cannot disown. But omnipotence, like all magical gifts, is double edged and dangerous; it can strengthen as well as harm its possessor and its receiver. The doctor's feeling of omnipotence can foster dependency, making a despot of the doctor and a child of the patient, or it can give the patient courage to learn control and free himself from fear.

6 The Healer's Battle

Claude lévi-strauss has categorized the shamanistic cures ordinarily described in non-Western cultures:

> These cures are of three types, which are not, however, mutually exclusive. The sick organ or member may be physically involved, through a manipulation or suction which aims at extracting the cause of the illness—usually a thorn, crystal, or feather made to appear at the opportune moment, as in tropical America, Australia, and Alaska. Curing may also revolve, as among the Arqucanians, around a sham battle, waged in the hut, and then outdoors, against harmful spirits. Or, as among the Navaho, the officiant may recite incantations and prescribe actions (such as placing the sick person on different parts of a painting traced on the ground with colored sands and pollens) which bear no direct relationship to the specific disturbance to be cured. In all these cases, the therapeutic method (which as we know is often effective) is difficult to interpret. When it deals directly with the unhealthy organ, it is too grossly concrete (generally, pure deceit) to be granted intrinsic value. And when it consists in the repetition of often highly abstract ritual, it

164

is difficult for us to understand its direct bearing on the illness. It would be convenient to dismiss these difficulties by declaring that we are dealing with psychological cures. But this term will remain meaningless unless we can explain how specific psychological representations are involved to combat equally specific physiological disturbances.

The features of illness that I have discussed and the function of the healer in dealing with them have given us some insight into how patients are returned to health by the healer, who does not deal directly with the specific features of the disease. Similarly, we have seen how curing the disease without paying attention to those other aspects of sickness might result in returning to normalcy a body part in a person who remains ill. However, to see the healer merely as one who hooks the conscious reasoning processes to the sensorimotor intelligence, spreads the cloak of his seeming omnipotence over the patient, provides a bridge between the patient's world of sickness and the healthy world, and offers the otherwise helpless patient an alternative method of controlling the body and the environment would be to miss the excitement and the drama in the act of healing.

Returning to the picture of the modes of healing presented by Lévi-Strauss, our examination of the factors involved has only partly explained why in disparate cultures the acts of healers are similar. In our culture, the seriously ill person feels small, frightened, and lost. The future is cloudy and filled with the apprehension of ignorance, reinforced by fears that are given the shape and substance of monsters. Nothing is sure; like a novice, the sick person must measure every step, with no confidence in his own ability. His control of his world and his body is slipping as mechanically, socially, and emotionally he becomes less agile. The specter of helplessness looms. His society begins to become distant as contacts are restricted by the physical restrictions of his illness and his own failing interest in others, as well as by the many who actually shun him. His own fears are enlarged by the fears others express by their pity, their overt statements, or even their silence. In all of this, one cannot exaggerate the ill person's fear of the progression to death. So strong is this fear that the fantasied progression to death—to nothingness—may be aroused in the patient by the news that his cholesterol is elevated!

Think back to the lightning flash of fear on being told of some bad finding in a medical checkup—a fear so quick and sharp and, in its intensity, short-lived that it can only have *preceded* actual thought about what the examination revealed. As a matter of fact, a few moments' thought may restore previous confidence and a sense of relative meanings and safety. But where did that flash of fear come from? It is as though the battle is always being fought, as though death always threatens. The fear is death, or is it? Since none of us have been there (as far as I know), why do we fear it? *Nothing*, however, is something we have all been, because we have all experienced the utter helplessness of infancy.

We know a great deal more about that helpless state in our sensorimotor memory than in our verbal memory. The progression to death, so feared by all, is, I believe, a fear of complete regression through helplessness to nothing. Now the battle is clearer. It is the constant battle within us. It is as if living and functioning did not continue forward in effortless flow, as if inertia must constantly be overcome. Even a muscle that is not used withers. Illness upsets the forces in favor of regression, and something is required to restore the balance of forces. In the healing rituals of non-Western societies, the dominant theme is battle. One healer sucks the disease from the supplicant— disease that is deadly to the patient, harmless to the healer. Another wages a vigorous sham battle with the spirits of the sickness on behalf of his patient. All these methods, says Lévi-Strauss, have in common the fact that the healer lives through the illness for the patient and emerges triumphant. The healer, in the sham battle of the healing ceremony, substitutes himself for the patient in a successful combat with the disease.

This "living through" is called "abreaction" in psychoanalytic terms and, if psychological cure is to be accomplished, it is essential that the patient abreacts under the protective wing of the therapist. As Lévi-Strauss points out, the psychoanalyst, in common with shamans in other cultures, has gone through the same experience in his own psychoanalysis.

But if abreaction by the healer is essential to healing, as I believe it to be, what place does this phenomenon have in the practice of the modern physician or surgeon?

Let us look briefly at the picture our culture has of its physicians. The country doctor was not only kindly and old; he was tired. All doctors are tired, so the saying goes. Patients tell me how tired I look when I am fresh as a daisy. They tell me how hard I work and how little sleep I get and, indeed, it is usually true. Doctors, especially younger ones, vie with each other as to who is the most tired. This pattern starts early in professional life, with interns working around the clock, exhausted by their labors. Fatigue is the real hallmark of the profession, because the struggle of our doctors is with death.

The image of such a struggle is beautifully conveyed

in a Norse legend, in which the Norse god Thor and his followers went to the castle of the giants of Juthunheim. A man of enormous strength, Thor was sure of his powers, but standing before the King of the giants, Utgard-Loki, he was dwarfed in stature by the King's huge size. "In what feats are you and your followers skilled," the King asked him, "for no one is permitted in the castle of the giants who does not, in something, exceed all other men."

Thor's companions were quickly bested at feats in which they excelled at home. Thor, asked what he would attempt, accepted a drinking match. The cupbearer offered a horn that Thor was told to empty in one draught. Though he tried mightily in one, then a second, and finally a third draught, he hardly succeeded in diminishing the volume of the liquid. The King, with open contempt, said that Thor seemed less a mighty man among the giants than he was reputed to be at home. Indeed, rather than waste the giants' time with tasks he could not achieve, Utgard-Loki asked if he would simply pick up the King's cat—a game so trifling that only the giant's children played it. Though Thor tried with all his strength, he succeeded merely in lifting one of the cat's paws from the ground.

Angered by his failures, Thor called on the King to have someone wrestle with him. The King said, "You will wrestle with that old crone, my nurse Elli. She has wrestled many no less strong than you." The wrinkled, toothless ancient entered the hall and Thor took hold of her. The more Thor leaned into his grip, the firmer she stood. The struggle was violent, but slowly Thor gave ground, and finally, his foot slipping, he was brought down on one knee. The King ordered them to stop.

The next morning, the King bade him good-bye. Thor felt ashamed and confessed that what grieved him most was that here he would be considered a man of little worth. "No," said the King. "Now I must tell you the truth. The horn from which you drank is connected to the ocean, and you lowered the water's level by a foot. And the cat is, in reality, the serpent that encircles the earth, and you almost broke her hold on the globe. But wrestling Elli was the most astonishing feat, for she is Old Age—and there is no man, now or ever, that death will not sooner or later lay low."

To reiterate, the mighty struggle of the doctor is with death. To the patient, the image of the doctor is that he has already struggled with death often—and has often won. Little wonder that doctors are tired. The abreaction of doctors is the living through of the struggle with death. Now think of the popular myths of modern medicine. (Although I use the word "myth," it is not because the picture is not based on fact, but because it involves a popular idea that would be necessary even if it were not supported by reality.)

The lights burning late at night in the hospital. The midnight vigil. Heroic operations and tired but selfless men and women at their task. Overwhelming odds, an inevitable struggle, and often success. And even when death wins, the struggle was admirable. ". . . There is no man, now or ever, that death will not sooner or later lay low." But a paradox presents itself. Death is inevitable, but death as an immediacy for all of us is denied by a contrary reality. As we saw in Chapter 2, for most of us in the Western world premature death is no longer imminent.

There are few things in our world with such wide personal, social, and cultural meanings as the loss of the imminence of premature death, a phenomenon unique to the generations born since the 1940s. For the lives of the young, "Time's wingèd chariot" no longer hurries, and the picking of rosebuds may be done at one's leisure. In essence, the young now have "limitless" time.

The changes that have occurred in the patterns of illness and death are not limited to the young. For the aged, too, the situation has changed. That we all die remains true, but the when and the how have shifted. What is "old" now? Only a little more than a generation ago, the seventy-year-old man was a relatively uncommon creature, considered old by himself and his family. The life expectancy of the aged has increased considerably. According to the actuarial tables, a person of sixty can now expect to live eighteen more years and a person of seventy has a life expectancy of eighty-two years. Although the human life span itself has not been significantly extended (even since Biblical times), more people are living longer than ever before.

Furthermore, and perhaps more important, the extension of life has meant the extension of *useful* life, functional life. The old among us may have many diseases (they usually do), but they often have little real illness. They may walk more slowly, or even with a cane, but they walk —and frequently to work. They may have glasses for their eyes and/or amplifiers for their ears, but they see and hear and function. Indeed, perhaps the most disabling thing in the lives of the old in recent times has been mandatory retirement at age sixty-five. Previously functional individuals are laid aside and frequently stagnate or even die from their uselessness. They have not been trained to combat the stresses of retirement or to meet the demand for new resources of creativity and growth. Biologically speaking, however, there is no such thing as standing still; there is only function or atrophy. But even that stagnation has begun to change. Sleek, expensive, silvery air-stream trailers, bought as retirement homes, streak back and forth across the nation, attached only transiently to electrical outlets in seemingly rootless denial of the gravity of aging. The image conjures up another similar picture of rootless youth hitch-hiking back and forth across the land like Thomas Pynchon's yo-yos, apparently equally free from gravity and beckoning all of us to freedom.

With the dramatic change in disease patterns during this century has come a change in the meaning of disability. We no longer automatically equate illness with disability, nor do we equate the disability of an organ with the disability of the whole man. Organ disability, in other words, does not mean functional disability. We replace the arm with pincers and the leg with a fancy stump. If a man cannot work at his original job, we retrain him. We train the blind to work in darkness and the deaf to transcribe stenotyping. As a culture, we have become dedicated to function.

This does not mean that disability has altogether disappeared. On the contrary, it is as widespread as ever. But there has been a decisive change, all too seldom recognized as such, in the direction from which disability comes. It is now more likely to arise from within a person or from his society (or his interaction with it) than from exogenous disease. Its origins are now primarily emotional, genetic (birth defects, etc.), or social.

For who are the disabled if not the nonfunctional? And who is less functional than the "misfit"—the alienated person, the addict, the alcoholic? Perhaps even our fabled "Corporation Man"—tightly jacketed by a set of rules and procedures that control the direction of his creative growth—might be called a disabled man. Creativity and growth are tender things. They emerge slowly and tentatively as we age and wither quickly if discouraged or stifled. But they are the stuff of which an era is made.

It would not be too difficult to show that the most common disabling diseases of our time—heart disease, certain cancers, and automobile accidents—are in themselves born of our culture. Coronary heart disease, our number-one cause of death and disability, seems to have risen to that prominence because of the habits of our society; a diet rich in fat and refined sugars; lack of physical exercise; some psychological factors (quickly accepted by laymen, but difficult to prove scientifically); and cigarette smoking. Automobile accidents, which are the leading cause of death among young adults, have now been shown to have their roots primarily in alcoholism and in the social and emotional life of drivers. (In a fatal automobile accident, the overwhelming probability is that one of the drivers will have been drinking and that he—because it is usually a male—will have had previous contact with social agencies, either because of alcohol or past misdemeanors.)

This is surely a new kind of disability, the roots of which are intertwined with the changes that have been wrought in the disease patterns of our generation. We have seen how the threat of imminent death in the young has left us as a meaningful probability and how the whole fabric of our culture is involved in the change. Old and young alike have become the beneficiaries of a new gift made possible by the changes in the patterns of disability. That gift is time—time in which to live. But the gift of time has not been without its price. The threat of a limited life imposes a corresponding demand, or need, to perform; the expectation of death imposes a sense of control and restraint. In this era the price exacted by the gift of time has often been a loss of that sense of control and a consequent anxiety or—even worse—a loss of the ability to function creatively.

It is interesting in this regard to contrast the present with the late eighteenth and early nineteenth centuries, when death at a young age was frequent. Tuberculosis, one of the most common causes of early death at that time, was greatly romanticized. The literature of the era was pervaded by a sense of the beauty of early death, and the pale, thin, languorous form of the tuberculosis patient became the fashion ideal of beauty, often copied even today. But what is of greatest interest is the fact that sufferers of tuberculosis were thought to be endowed with some special genius. Their drive to produce seemed enormous, as though a strong wind blew within, hastening them to their artistic task and fanning the flame of their creativity. But they all knew of their impending death (including some who didn't die, almost to their disappointment), and I think that knowledge imposed the final deadline against which they all worked so feverishly.

I know a young graduate student who had been pursuing his studies in a dilatory manner. Then he was found to have a fatal disease. When informed of this, he suddenly began to perform and finish his work in order to become something in the limited time left to him. The demand to perform was imposed by the diagnosis of imminent death. How many of us have not played the game of, "What would you do if you knew you were going to die in —?" Generally, rather than playing out their lives in pursuit of futile games, people feel the need for accomplishment in the short time left to them. For some, accomplishment may be professional; for others, spiritual or familial, some goal to give the void a personal meaning.

A sense of time develops as we grow up. A child's

total concern seems to be with the moment. An hour is meaningless; next week may be a forever away. A real sense of time begins to appear in adolescence. This is also the period when fantasies of early death occur. "I know that I'm going to die young" is so commonly heard among adolescents that it must be considered as an expression of group feeling rather than of unique individual experience. As a cultural phenomenon this feeling stems from the knowledge that in earlier periods it has happened: the list of talented men who died young is long. Its attraction for youth, however, lies more in its beauty as an idea—a short, postadolescent catharsis, then death. One has done important work, given the world one's talents, and then, before being challenged by continued existence, one expires. What would one do if one had to go on—and on and on?

The fantasy of premature death in modern adolescents may be seen as a response to the tensions arising from the loosening of parental control. It is also, in my view, a response to the perception that premature death is in fact among the unlikeliest of eventualities.

One might stop at this point and ask whether the young know that they are freed from the threat of death. I think they do because, despite the stories of their parents, grandparents, and the literature, as they look around them their friends are all alive. A few have been sick—even very sick—but virtually all are alive.

Some people use the threat of nuclear holocaust to deny that the imminence of death is lost for the young. To me, however, that evidence offers more support than denial of my point. The "bomb" with all its horrors is an abstraction, a conception of death called up to meet the need for the threat, but with none of the immediacy of knowing somebody young who is dying. Whether or not we wish to acknowledge them consciously, the facts of life that are known to us influence our behavior. The absence of death is one of the facts of life to the young.

Now, while the gift of time must surely be marked as a great blessing, the perception of time as stretching out endlessly before us is somewhat threatening. Many of us function best under deadlines and tend to procrastinate when time limits are not set. Time limits are controls, and some controls seem to make people more comfortable. Thus this previously unquestioned boon—the extension of life and the removal of the threat of premature death—carries with it unexpected anxiety: the anxiety of an unlimited future.

In the young, it seems to me, the sense of limitless time has apparently imparted not a feeling of limitless opportunity, but rather increased stress and anxiety to be added to the anxiety that results from other modern freedoms: personal mobility, a wide range of occupational choice, and independence from limitations of class and family patterns.

A few years ago it seemed to me that the anxiety born of the new freedom from death and the consequent need to choose how to live was at least one component of the open rebellion among the young in the 1960s. Times have changed and rebellion has been replaced by conformity, despite the fact that the immediacy of death has not returned. What irony, however.

Death has returned, but now in symbolic form. This is shown by the present romance with death and dying evident in the way the literature on the subject has been clasped to the bosom of the young. College courses on death abound and are extremely popular. Even high schools have courses and seminars on death. Books on death and dying have become best-sellers! At a time when we have staved off death as never before, we are suddenly obsessed with it. When we no longer have the real threat—imminent, early death—to prod us on through life, we call for the vision of it anyway.

Death, as has been repeatedly pointed out in many contexts, is essential to living and life. Here we see the need both for the symbol of mortality and the threat that there may be no tomorrow. Death moves time from abstract infinity to concrete reality. But, alas, symbol or no, premature death is not imminent and the problem of filling a long life with meaning remains. Women provide the most clear-cut example of the way in which the pattern of our lives has been influenced by the changes in the pattern of our diseases in past decades. Women have gained time directly, by the extension of their own lives, and indirectly, from the gains of their children. It may be said that one of the major social changes in this century has been the emergence of women as a social force—an emergence that might not have been possible were it not for the survival of the young. Because it no longer takes seven full-term pregnancies to produce five living children, and five living children to produce three adults, the time required for women to discharge their biological function has been markedly reduced. They are free to pursue their own non-maternal functions very much more quickly. Late marriage becomes feasible (not merely as a birth-control device as in mainland China) because there will still be adequate time for childbearing. But late marriage also means individual development—college and careers—and that means aspirations apart from marriage. When frustrated (or "unperceived"), those unfulfilled aspirations mean boredom and unhappiness and the myriad problems for the modern healthy woman that have come under popular discussion in recent years.

The difficulty in handling the newly won time is best demonstrated by women because they have been assaulted by the advance from all sides. Birth control made illegitimate pregnancy an unnecessary absurdity many years ago, but still such pregnancies continued. They can be regarded as self-induced disabilities—accidents only in the loosest sense of the term. An unwanted pregnancy, even in this day of legal abortion, serves to remind women of their (no longer) "secondary" role and frequently even to cripple their aspirations through guilt.

Legitimate pregnancies, too, can be utilized to avoid the promise and decrease the threat of an unlimited future. Coming too soon, or too close together, they can convince a woman (in denial of fact) that her biological function must necessarily override her own personal (or even marital) creative needs. Similarly, a woman who lives in constant fear of her children's impending death from every little fever (despite the informed boredom of her pediatrician about the same fever) raises her family without giving heed to herself as a person. In times past, suffering from female diseases could be a middle-years career for women, but they, too, have gone the way of infectious diseases— very uncommon or easily treatable. Thus the children, few in number and healthy, grow up, leaving her healthy, young (by modern standards)—and frequently useless.

If all of this were not true, could the woman's movement of today have such wide goals and aspirations?

The aged again serve to clarify the issues I have been discussing, primarily because they have been freed by the passage of time and by their own aging from some of the problems that face the young. Oddly, they do not have such problems because they do not perceive them as problems. They know that they are going to die, and it doesn't seem to bother them much. I have had conversations with old people in which they discussed their approaching death with great calm while their children seated nearby nearly fainted in distress. Being a burden—that is truly frightening; being an invalid and being unable to take care of oneself causes real and well-based anxiety. But the fears of unlimited time have been removed. Now, great blessing, there isn't enough time. The aged have terrible disability problems. Disability is a real threat, but even so the aged are apparently safe from themselves. When disability comes, it will come from outside themselves. (Unfortunately, of course, that is not always true. The aged are still their own worst enemy, along with the rest of us. Some are disabled by diseases that do not affect others in the same way. But at least, unlike the young, they have more outside themselves on which to place the blame.)

I have used the phrase "changes in the patterns of disease" in speaking of what many people would refer to as changes in our general cultural climate. I have done so because I believe that in some measure our new cultural ills can be linked to the prodigious successes the medical profession has achieved in our lifetime. I think it fair, then, since physicians have been an intimate part—though by no means the only one—of the revolution in disease, that we look to them for some recognition of our new problems and some indication of the direction in which all of us must move toward their solutions.

In medicine, there are, and always have been, two

basic priorities: the defense against imminent death and the defense against disability.

Priority One thinking, the defense against imminent death, operates properly in the period immediately following a heart attack, during and right after surgery, immediately after serious trauma, and during war or similar situations. The excitement of Priority One thinking is the basis for the continued popularity of many medical television shows—the accident, the speeding paramedic squad, the operating-room scene where the camera pans from the cardiac monitor to the nurse's hands passing an instrument from her tray to the deft fingers of the surgeon. The same kind of thinking pervades emergency rooms, volunteer ambulance services, and all the situations where humans seem separated from death by one fragile heartbeat. And Priority One thinking is in the dreams of everyone who wants to be a doctor—the medical expression, perhaps, of the universal Walter Mitty fantasy.

Now the basic threat in Priority One thinking, death, has not changed over the years; it has simply become less probable, and among the young (except for accidents) uncommon indeed. Nevertheless, death is death—an end to life. And because nothing can change the awesome finality that is at the core of the threat of death, it has become possible to maintain artificially the belief that the importance of Priority One thinking is just as great as it ever was. This in turn allows such thinking to be carried over into an area like that of the infectious diseases, where the threat of death has in fact become virtually nonexistent. Thus we frequently see among physicians, as well as among patients, an overreaction to minor infectious diseases, apparently based on the fear that the "minor" will become a "major"—that a cold, say, will become pneumonia. Yet few besides the aged or otherwise terminally ill die from pneumonia. There is that old saw about a patient with a cold who says to his doctor, "What if it turns into pneumonia?" The doctor is said to have answered, "Better if it were pneumonia. *That* I can cure." If there were no antibiotics, it would be different. If there were no hospitals and operating rooms and surgeons and ambulances—but for most of us in the Western world, there *are* all these things. Just as the complex whole of our society seems to have changed our disease pattern, so the complex whole of our society has changed the meaning of potentially fatal diseases. (Again, in discussing the change in the meaning of disease, just as in discussing the change in the pattern of disease, concepts such as the ones I have been using are justified only so long as the society remains stable.)

As a physician, I must confess that there is a certain romance in Priority One defense-against-death beliefs. There is admittedly an excitement in seeing the red streaks that run up the arm of a patient whose hand infection has begun to spread (a morbid excitement, perhaps, but that is a doctor's work). And to the patient, there is a very real fear—fear of illness and pain and even death. But the excitement all ends at the drugstore, when simply purchased tablets promptly end the threat in the majority of instances. (Untreated, the disease is dangerous; but then so is a car without brakes.)

Priority Two of medical care is the defense against disability. We have seen how the direction of disability for the young has been changed by the conquest of the infectious diseases as well as by recent advances. But curiously, in this most difficult task in medicine—defense against disability—the burden has increased. The young who do not die grow old and suffer the diseases for which we still have no cure: arthritis, diabetes, heart disease, cancer. Children with previously fatal diseases now live disabled lives, needing continuing care.

This priority—defense against disability—is based upon the classical functions of physicians: to comfort and to relieve. Both are inadequate for patient and doctor alike in the present era of the expectation of cure. It is far easier to escape to simpler, more basic fears, to reduce the anxiety and the danger that time has given us by maintaining the belief that premature death is imminent and beyond our control.

The "romance" of acute disease, stubbornly maintained in the face of steadily mounting fact, can be explained in several ways. For the patient, the sense of an outward "threat" saves him from having to recognize that the real threat is life and that the real source of disability is within himself. As for the physician, he, too, is a person with the same fears as his patient. But there are other reasons why physicians need to keep the compact with their patients and maintain the "romance" of acute disease, the importance of Priority One defense-against-death thinking in the face of all evidence to the contrary. All the long and continuing training of physicians has been, and (sadly) still is, oriented toward solutions to Priority One problems: the defense against imminent death, the treatment of acute disease, and the protection against imminent danger. But as we have seen, these are no longer the greatest dangers facing us, or those for which we require the most help. Dealing with life is difficult and painful, and that is most often where our physicians fail to help us. They have solutions, but not to our most pressing problems. If one has no solutions to the real problems of this world, it is easier to continue to maintain, no matter how artificially, the primacy of the problems for which one does have solutions.

Life is the problem—providing meaning and fulfillment, depth and happiness in life. These tasks, requiring a whole lifetime, are beyond the function of the physician. It is true, as we have seen, that he can make the job of living harder by maintaining fear of the body and fear of death. And he can make the job easier by teaching how to live with the body, how to surmount illness and conquer disability. Creating happiness is not the work of physicians. That task must be achieved by each of us alone, as it has always been. But even leaving out happiness, doctors are needed by people not only for their diseases. To whom can we turn when we are overwhelmed, when our need is greater than love alone can supply, or when loss denies us love's comfort and support? The "melancholy, long, withdrawing roar" of the Sea of Faith is even more distant than when Matthew Arnold wrote his poem *Dover Beach*.

"What is a doctor's job?" I asked a patient, a middle-aged woman who was in the hospital with rheumatic heart disease. "To keep me alive—and more," she said. "Because especially now, I don't believe in God anymore really and truly. So the doctor's job is one that never existed before—far beyond any of the others. There were some gods that took care of everything, and there was Jesus. . . . There was once another world, but since I don't believe in it any more, for me the doctor is now God. . . . All the things that were asked of gods, essentially what were they? Even if the Aztecs let the blood out, it was to give more life. Now there is only the doctor to protect me from the things around us."

7 Overcoming the Fear of Death

INCREASINGLY THE TERMINALLY ILL or the aged will find their wishes concerning the manner of their death respected by a more understanding society or protected by a more merciful law. It is even possible that some arrangement will evolve to enable a life burdened by pain or disease to be ended by the sanctioned act of others.

The problems of the dying, along with their protection and their rights, find an expanding interest whose expression varies from the large number of attempts at effective statutory regulation through swelling membership in euthanasia societies to the now huge number of courses, seminars, and publications devoted to the subject.

I assume that change will occur because so many other aspects of the private lives of individuals, once rigidly determined by social structure, have become the right of each person to determine. With this change we shall be faced by a far greater problem than securing a peaceful death for the small minority of people who, on their deathbeds, are assaulted by an overwhelming technology. We shall be faced by the challenge of dying well, of living fully and without fear that last phase of life.

New family styles are proposed and tried every day—

indeed, the family itself seems like some besieged medieval town with both attackers and defenders fighting with ideological zeal. Yet most of us know that some form of enduring relationship is as desirable as it is hard to achieve. However, the freedom to dissolve a marriage, live in a commune, live in threes, fours, or whatever, puts the entire burden of maintaining the relationships on the people involved. No longer can the individual point to an inflexible law as the reason he or she is forced to live in an unhappy union, dreaming of the joy that could be his or hers if only. . . . Sexual freedom has also been won but appears not to have brought quite so much freedom from ourselves as seemed promised. Here again, as long as social strictures existed, each person could blame the world around him for his inability to rise above his inhibitions. But now everyone must accept the fault for his own meaningless sexual activity, joyless coupling, or the failure to demonstrate love.

In the same manner modern geographic and social mobility, along with wide educational and vocational opportunity, has placed on each person the responsibility for his or her own growth. Beyond the constraints of the social structure lies the challenge for all of us to attain our greatest potential. (It may be argued that, despite the newfound social freedom, we are locked into our self-stunting behavior by unconscious conflicts laid down so early in life that their solution, without psychotherapeutic treatment, is beyond our control. This, too, is in question as recent trends in psychology suggest that it is an oversimplification of the human condition to view an adult as merely a big person with a five-year-old at the controls. Similarly, the behaviorist belief that everything we do results exclusively from our conditioning seems an uncharitable, if not downright simplistic, perspective of humanity.)

Thus we may assume that with the success of the right-to-die movement, the manner of our own deaths will come increasingly under our own control. The challenge will not be to deny that fate exists in the form of aging or fatal disease; rather, it will be to die well within the constraints of those same fates.

Just as every other social constraint against which we have bridled has made it difficult for us to realize ourselves and our strengths, so too has it protected us against our weaknesses. The situation here is no different.

Once a new definition of human fairness and mercy has freed some terminal patients from their pain and from the wires and tubes connected to machines that contravene natural law, the definition of what constitutes an extreme case will begin to change. It is probable that we shall recognize that what is an extreme or unendurable death is a personal matter and not for others alone to determine. Accordingly, we shall allow each person to determine what is for him a just and fair death. We recognize at once what a predicament this would put us in—how much responsibility each of us would bear for calling upon our inner and outer resources at a time of weakness, sadness, and pain. Perhaps it is from this recognition that our present modes of dealing with the dying have protected us.

As always, each increase in personal freedom brings with it the difficult problem of learning to use it wisely. In liberalizing abortion laws, we argued that no mother should have to bear a deformed child because she took thalidomide or had German measles. Neither did we wish an unwanted child born into a home where it would certainly suffer merely from the fact of its birth. But once liberalized abortion laws were passed, we found them being extended as part of the expansion of personal liberty. The new freedom requires that a woman accept as hers, and hers alone, the ultimate responsibility for deciding whether to kill her fetus, even when her health or its health is not threatened.

The situation of the dying is different in some respects, however. If one is in conflict about sex, marriage, or abortion, one may simply avoid the behavior that produces the conflict. On the other hand, no one can avoid death. Increasingly these days people die in old age, aware well ahead that death is approaching. Moreover, for the great majority of us, confronting the problem of dying well does not have to wait for changes in the laws and customs, although current social attitudes and legal restraints prevent us from realizing how great are our existing options.

There are several obstacles that stand in the way of dying well—of the "good death," in terms similar to the "good marriage," the "good family," the "good birth." It seems to me that the obstacles to a "good death" for the dying or for those who care for the dying lie in the prevalent attitudes toward death of passivity, resistance or denial, and fear.

I want to emphasize that in this chapter I am speaking of the process of dying, rather than of death itself, and it is a process in which the dying person can take an active part. I am concerned primarily with the terminally ill adult, not with the young or with suicide or sudden death in the previously healthy. This discussion is concerned with the vast majority of us who will die of disease in our older years. Almost every experienced clinician knows that some people die better than others, that some families deal better with the problem than others, and that the differences cannot be explained solely by differences in the terminal disease or the nature of the treatment.

In the scenario of dying, many people, many lives, and many intense and different emotions are involved. The rest of the world goes on, but around the dying person time slows or comes to a halt. The passage of time, the orderly progression of life for the other actors, will not resume until long after the death. To see the dying person as only an essential prop for this drama, merely a significant piece of scenery, is an error, the same error of understanding that occurs when one considers himself or others as necessarily passive in the process of dying—dragged to death by disease or infirmity as a child drags a doll. We do not like to conceive of death in such passive terms, exemplified by the lines from the *Iliad*: "miserable mortals who, like leaves, at one moment flame with life, eating the produce of the land, and at another moment weakly perish." Indeed, we do identify this attitude with the miserable of the world. Television has projected into our homes endless pictures of the miserable, the starving, the war-torn— masses of humanity who, in our inability to help, we always picture as masses, not as individuals. It is as though their bodily deprivations denied them the luxury of individuality and hence we do not see them as determining, in any active sense, what their stance toward death will be. That is not the fate we wish for ourselves. We prefer an attitude of resistance toward death.

For some the only acceptable alternative to passivity in the face of death is resistance. Dylan Thomas's famous lines are symbolic.

> Do not go gentle into that good night.
> Old age should burn and rave
>   at close of day;
> Rage, rage against the dying
>   of the light.

But to whom does Thomas refer in these lines? Himself?
No, he is speaking of his father.

> And you, my father, there
>   on the sad height,
> Curse, bless, me now with your
>   fierce tears, I pray.
> Do not go gentle into that good night.
> Rage, rage against the dying
>   of the light.

The call to resist death, then, comes as much from
those around the dying person as from within him. From
within the person, the resistance to death is born of the
habit of a lifetime. Life itself is a constant battle to live,
to overcome fatigue and the impulse to stop simply because the struggle can be so tiring. Among the well the
drive to live seems based on the biology of the organism.
The child and the young adult are propelled along by the
force of the drive: Young people spring back to vitality
quickly from even the most severe illness. But with increasing age the return to health seems to require increased
work, until in the aged almost volition alone explains the
effort. The habits of a lifetime become a part of the character of the individual and the resistance to dying an expression of the ingrained habit of living.

I have a patient who has severe emphysema and who is

quite old. His life was spent in menial work, and his family has fallen away from around him—victims of disease or strife. In his old age he is beginning to achieve stature in his own eyes by, it would seem, the very fact of his survival. Each visit to my office records his achievement: he is still living despite his infirmities, besting the world around him as never before by the simple fact of remaining alive. Most of us know people who have gone from reticence about telling how old they are to pride at being so old, sometimes even adding a few years in the telling of it; their resistance to death arises from the vanity of remaining alive.

As we saw in the Dylan Thomas poem, the resistance to death also comes from the world around the dying person. We belong to others. The people whom we love and who love us have a claim on us. At no time does that claim seem so urgent as at the bedside of the dying. "Isadore," said my Aunt Celia to her husband as he lay on a stretcher in the hospital corridor, mortally ill, "you promised me that I could die first." What choice did my uncle have but to get better? A promise is a promise.

Children need their parents; spouses need each other. There is so much yet to be said and done. Sibling conflicts and jealousies that date back to the nursery and that have continued over the years in defiance of mortality are suddenly chilled by the tolling of the bell. (I once made a house call on two ancient spinster sisters who lived together, one of whom was dying. As I went toward the room of the sick woman, her sister stopped me to say, "Don't believe a word she says. She lies a lot; she always has.") If only the dying person will fight, resist, deny the tolling bell, things can be made right again, or at least resolved. (It matters little here, but it is sad that when reprieves do occur, people seldom take advantage of the gift of time to resolve their conflicts or bring peace among themselves—not never, fortunately, but not often enough.)

Frequently, the call from others for the dying person to fight death results in his isolation. He finds himself in a situation where he must protect his loved ones from the fact of his own approaching death. He cannot tell the others about his pain or weakness; he must constantly display his fighting attitude even when there is little fight left. The family, too, must keep up the front, sometimes going from doctor to doctor, from one kind of treatment to another, always attributing the fighting attitude to the patient, not to their own denial of the inevitable.

Here we can see how the attitude of resistance to death borders on denial of death. Denial of death doesn't have a very good reputation these days. In these times everybody is supposed to know everything and everything must be put into words—or so it sometimes seems to me. What a pity! Denial of the unpleasant is a universal psychological mechanism that can be extremely useful. Every physician has seen patients successfully use denial to protect themselves from painful truths apparently so obvious that denial should be impossible.

Denial seems to have fallen into disrepute, perhaps because it goes against the fashionable doctrine of truth-telling: doctors are enjoined from all sides to tell the truth to patients. In part this trend is a reaction to the tendency of some physicians not to communicate with their patients and to imply that patients don't have the intelligence to understand, but I think that this is not the whole story. Despite the current rejection of the value of denial, it remains an extremely common human mode for dealing with the unpleasant, the unacceptable, or the painful. It is one of the paradoxes of this overrational age (for which you may read overly analytic) that people behave as though speech and reason can stop the mind from using such an inherently biological defense. Thus speech and verbiage themselves can give the illusion that everything is out in the open while actually serving the ends of denial—the denial of feeling and of fate, if nothing else. No matter— the illusion provides the opportunity to explore the problem posed by the rejection of denial, a matter of great importance in the care of the sick and the dying.

The basic problem presented by denial is that a lie is involved—telling oneself an untruth. The classic instance is the patient with cancer on a cancer ward who tells the visitor how lucky he, the patient, is to be well; after all, everybody else on the ward has cancer. We stand in awe of such a belief in the face of a constantly assaulting reality. Unfortunately, for the denial to remain intact the onlookers must also lie—the family, the nurses, the doctor, and all others who know the truth. They must all watch their words and be discreet in both conversation and chart notations. With the burden goes responsibility. The use of denial by a patient means that those around him must share in the responsibility of protecting him from pain. I believe it is that responsibility that has caused denial to be a disvalued mode for dealing with death. It may be uncharitable of me, but I think that many people nowadays, particularly young people (from whom the greatest objection to the use of denial is heard), do not like heavy responsibility resting on them.

Where do we hear the objection to denial, and in what form? We do not hear the objection at the bedside, in the actual setting of patient care. There it is difficult to teach young doctors and nurses how to tell the truth. In that setting of sickness and misery it is too easy to fall in with the family's or the patient's desire (perceived or spoken) not to know the painful facts. At the bedside it takes a full acceptance of one's responsibility in order to bring difficult words to the lips, and a full inner realization that to tell someone of his cancer or impending death is not the same as giving him his cancer or causing his death. Rather, we hear the criticism of denial at meetings, seminars, or discussions about medical care, far removed from the scene of the dying and voiced primarily by healthy laymen. The farther away from the bedside we get, the more highly valued is truth-telling and the more disvalued is denial. In such discussions physicians experienced in patient care often find themselves on the defensive. They are accused of not telling the truth to patients, of hiding behind the mystique of the profession. I have been in many such conversations at formal meetings and over cocktails that puzzled and troubled me, just as they have my clinical colleagues. Most doctors walk away feeling that further discussion is pointless, since laymen just don't seem to understand. Naturally, the laymen walk away with the same feeling: doctors just don't understand and that's why they behave the way they do. Such misunderstandings imply that there is no common basis for discussion. In such dialogues with laymen I usually think that if they had to take care of patients they wouldn't assume that sick people think just as they do—that the sick were the same as the healthy. I suspect that the laymen walk away saying to themselves that I am just another arrogant doctor who thinks that he has the right to decide what other people should know or should be told. Moreover, the seeming lack of objection to denial on the part of the patient or the family implies that it isn't the patient who initiates denial but rather the physician. And though surely physicians sometimes do initiate it, most often denial starts in the patient.

There, I believe, lies part of the truth. For denial to be an effective defense, people must deny its existence. In other words, the healthy may have to deny the utility of denial for it to be useful for them when sick. But more is involved. The terms "hierarchical" or "elitist" are often applied to physicians, especially by the radical movement in medicine, which frequently attacks the "medical establishment" in just those terms. When doctors are viewed as elitists, the complaint that they don't tell the whole truth to patients means that they are behaving as if they "knew better than" their patients—as if they were superior and the patients inferior. If the doctors protest, saying that the patient is dependent and needs them to function the way they do, the doctor is accused of not having a "right head," of a kind of residual medical colonialism.

I have little hope of escaping from such labels, but a brief examination of the word "equality" is necessary in connection with medicine. Equality and inequality are highly charged political words, and medicine, when it comes to the care of an individual sick person, is not politics (although systems of medical care may be political, just as the relationship between the sexes may be political but, hopefully, having sex is not). Thus these words are irrelevant, but they cannot be dismissed lightly. It must be apparent from what has gone before in this book that the sick are different from the well. Transiently, in respect to their ability to function they are not the equal of the well. Because of that "inequality" they must depend on the moral burden their need puts on the well to care for them until they are "equal" again.

The relationship is founded on moral, not legal, terms. In moral terms the doctor is bound to the sick person. In such terms he can be seen as the subject as well as the master. It is the nature of that bond that is difficult to put into words. It has technical, personal, emotional, social, and ethical aspects, and the boundaries of each category are fuzzy and overlap the others. The bond goes both ways, and its meaning to both patient and doctor changes through time. It is, in other words, very complex and poorly understood, but its basis lies in the moral nature of man. For a world that consistently shifts what is moral into the legal and the technical realms, the relationship is inexplicable without using words like inequality, associated with a distasteful sense of elitism that confuses the issue. When such an intimate and powerful, though transient, responsibility of one person for another is at issue, words such as "inequality" or "elitism" help doctors avoid the necessity for taking responsibility. Where the bond between patient and doctor is recognized as being moral, the words "elitism," "hierarchy," or even "paternalism" do not apply.

Perhaps it could be put another way that is less emotionally charged. In the doctor-patient relationship the sick person needs the doctor. The doctor also needs the sick person. The doctor needs patients to make a living, to practice his skills, to increase his self-esteem as well as to have their help in the very process of their medical care. However, all those needs can be met by any patient. The doctor's feelings may be hurt somewhat if a particular patient leaves him, but that will be the extent of his injury. The patient needs the doctor to get better. Perhaps any doctor will do equally well to make him better, but the patient does not usually see it that way. The patient, however, is much more liable to injury from the relationship than the doctor. If the doctor leaves the patient during the course of treatment, the patient will be the worse off for the doctor's departure (or so they both usually feel). The point is supported by the fact that a patient is not liable under the law if he leaves a doctor but a doctor can be sued for malpractice if he leaves a patient during the patient's care unless arrangements have been made for a substitute. Where no such arrangements are made, it is called abandonment, which is a serious charge.

To demonstrate both the essentially temporary nature of the relationship and its basis in human need, we could give as an example a situation where the patient is a cardiologist with a broken leg. He needs the orthopedist (the only one available) and is totally dependent on the orthopedist's skill. The day after the leg is in the cast and the cardiologist is feeling well again, the orthopedist has a heart attack. Now the orthopedist needs the cardiologist (the only one available) and is totally dependent on his skill. Both are equal in the eyes of the law, and both have equal intelligence, income, height, training, background, and so on ad infinitum. But, when each, in his turn, is sick, he needs the other in the special way the sick need the well. Equality has nothing to do with it.

Having said all that and having acknowledged that denial seems to have fallen from favor, it is still an extremely common attitude in both the dying and their families. The ways in which denial operates are many, and its power to protect is wondrous. Sometimes the person simply fails to hear what has been said. Unpleasant facts are told and minutes later the person speaks and acts as if nothing had occurred. I remember telling a patient with normal hearing some bad news. She kept saying,

"I'm sorry, I can't hear you," after each louder repetition. I finally had to yell. Sometimes only selected parts of the conversation are remembered, and at other times the patient or family make up a whole new set of facts to fill the gaps. Denial being a process occurring through time, the person may gradually remember what was told him over a period of days as he becomes able to accept the news. On other occasions the patient clearly tells the doctor what he must *not* be told. It doesn't require much practical experience before physicians have encountered all the various forms in which denial presents itself. Most doctors feel that the patient's right to deny is as basic as his right to be told the truth. The fundamental right of patients in such matters is to have their wishes respected whether their doctor agrees with them or not. The fact that denial has become unpopular or that it is a mode that I do not really like seems irrelevant in the presence of a dying person who has chosen to deny knowledge of that fate.

Often the family tells the doctor that the patient must not be told bad news because they "couldn't take it." In those situations the doctor is not sure who cannot take what and it becomes necessary to make delicate inquiries as to where the problem lies. It is inherently a bad situation, it seems to me, when the family knows something the patient does not. A conspiracy of silence develops that may loosen family bonds at a time when closeness is most important. Perhaps the most painful situations are those in which the dying patient knows the truth but the rest of the family either thinks that the patient does not know or refuses to let the patient talk about his illness or fears ("There's no need to talk about it. You know the doctors said that everything will be all right. . . ."). When that happens, to the distress of the illness is added the loneliness of unburdened fears—not only fears about illness or death, but also fears and problems concerning the children's future, the spouse's life ahead, all the details in the lives of those who will be left after the person dies.

A patient, at her own request, had been discharged from the hospital so that she could die at home. She knew her situation fully and was in good control. Her children also knew that she was dying. Because her husband had long-standing incapacitating mental disease (manic-depressive), the oldest son was acting as head of the family and had decided not to tell his father because of fear about what problems might follow. Not long before she died, she asked to see me at her home because, I was told, she had become so weak. But that was not the reason. She was upset that the children would not tell her husband that she was dying, and she wanted me to tell him. I sat in the kitchen with the husband, whom I had never met before, and explained what was happening, but I avoided the word "dying." When I went back to her room and reported the conversation to her, she said, "You didn't really tell him." I called the husband in, sat him on a chair facing her, and said, "Mr. Bartlett, your wife wants you to know that she is dying. . . . And she really is." She was immensely relieved. Just before I left, I asked her about her symptoms to make sure that she was comfortable. To questions about pain, nausea, and so forth, she replied in the negative. "What bothers you most, Ellen?" I asked. "What they did to him Sunday when they wouldn't tell him."

The depression in patients that commonly occurs after the diagnosis of a fatal disease seems to stem in part from the conspiracy of silence. The physician can be a great help by simply making it clear to the patient that he is available for open and direct conversation if that is desired. He need not necessarily force a conversation but can show his availability with such words as, "You know, you can talk to me about this whole problem whenever you wish; words like 'death' or 'cancer' won't scare me away." What is said is not as important as opening the lines of communication.

Each doctor has, or must develop, his own style. It is easy for someone who never has to look the dying patient in the eyes or who isn't responsible for day-to-day care to tell doctors the "right way." It is another thing when you are there.

My own preference is to try to find out what the patient wants to know and to supply that much information truthfully. I am uncomfortable with an open lie. Determining what the patient wants to know may mean asking directly, indirectly, or metaphorically, or by sensing feelings. Uncomfortable, awkward feelings in a patient's hospital room proclaim unmistakably—louder than words— that an unanswered question must be dealt with. At such times conversation is stilted and often about inconsequential matters such as the weather or sports. When people make small talk in the presence of big problems, it is usually not that they don't want to talk about the important issues, but that they don't know how. Often the family or even physicians are afraid of saying "the wrong thing," so they say nothing. The patient takes the cue and the silence goes on—and so does the loneliness.

It is certainly true that many physicians do not give enough information. They are afraid of telling the patient too much because that will lead to questions that they cannot answer or predictions to which they are unwilling to commit themselves. However, I believe that what the patient wants to know can be supplied more easily than most doctors think. Furthermore, the honest answer, "I don't know," to some of the big questions does not preclude answers to questions about pain, disability, costs, nursing, and so on. After all, what is the truth? Is it always the same for patient and doctor? Do we want the doctor to unburden himself or to unburden the patient? In the following quotation Dr. Thomas Addis, a noted Scottish physician, is speaking of a patient with a kidney disease that is sometimes fatal, but his comments are equally pertinent whenever death or tragedy lurks in the shadow of disease.

The first question that arises is whether we should show the patient [the evidence that may or may not indicate a marked worsening of the disease]. In this particular instance we would not only not let him see [the evidence]; we would take pains to see that no one else told him about it. Nor would we tell his mother, because to tell her would only be an indirect way of telling him. We would tell no one. The reason is that telling gains nothing, but may lose some of that freedom from anxiety that is an element in the patient's well being and a factor in determining the rate of progression of the disease. It may seem as though we were here advocating that the patient be deceived, or at least that certain truths be kept from him. That is not the case. What is being concealed is our fear that the change in the urine may indicate the beginning of the degenerative stage, but it is a fear that is concealed, not a truth. It is still quite possible that these signs will disappear and that everything be as it was before. In that event, would it really have been honest to have had the patient look at that [telltale test] tube?

To him it would necessarily have been an inescapable brute fact, unmitigated by that doubt as to its permanency and meaning that is given by the physician's experience. Honesty is not easy. It is certainly not achieved by the process, so comfortable to us all, of getting rid by confession of all our wandering fancies. Honesty with patients requires thought and discipline and effort. It has its negative as well as its positive side and requires silence as well as communication. Patients have a right to be very sure that when they ask we will tell them all we know. That is essential if they are to be kept from anxiety. But, while we must share our knowledge with them, we must not ask them to participate in our fears. These are our burdens and we must carry them alone.

In considering what doctors tell patients, it must be remembered that physicians are, like anyone else, extremely uncomfortable when they feel helpless. Therefore, they may at times go to great lengths to avoid telling the patient something that says, in essence, that there is no more that they can do to stop the progress of the disease or to avoid death. But patients understand, perhaps better than physicians, that doctors are only human and that medicine has limitations; not all patients can be cured or saved. The occasions when nothing can be done to help the dying patient, or any patient, are rare in the extreme. The physician who sees his role only as the curer of disease or the battler against death is often helpless; the physician who knows that his function is to help the sick to the limit of his ability is almost always able to offer something. In his care the sick are protected from helplessness, fear, and loneliness, agonies that are worse than death.

The attitudes toward death that have been discussed

—passivity, resistance, and denial—all seem at one time or another to be fostered by the physician and the apparatus of medical care. Rarely is the care of the very sick solely the dyadic concern of patient and doctor. The cast of characters around the dying patient is large, and the action usually takes place in that most complex of settings, the modern hospital. Merely meeting the intricate scheduling involved in efficiently running the X-ray department, the laboratory, the special procedures, or the operating room requires enormous compliance on the part of the patients and staff alike. Here passivity is wanted. That patient succeeds best who merely lies down and does what he or she is told. The models for such behavior are those hospital wards run by old-time surgical head nurses. Woe betide the patient who still wants pain shots on the third postoperative day. First comes the lecture on the dangers of drug addiction, followed by the sermon on doing for oneself that can make a corporation president feel like a draftee. When it comes to caring for the desperately sick those nurses are superb, but encouragement of patient individuality is not their thing.

Similarly, the attitude of resistance to disease and death permeates the atmosphere of the hospital. The staff wants patients to fight to get better. They want them up and walking before the rubber is out of their legs—bravely marching up and down the hall pushing the ubiquitous wheeled intravenous poles. (Sometimes when I see such patients walking along with the IV tubing draped around them, I am reminded of the astronauts walking in space attached to the spaceship and to life by the umbilical cord from the space suit.) Tasteless meals must be forced down by patients to whom the very sight of food is nauseating. The hospital, whatever else it may be, is a tomorrow place.

Tomorrow will be a better day; fight for it. Patients do this for themselves, for the staff, for the visitors; it is expected and it is necessary. The markers of resistance to disease are not grand philosophical slogans, but body markers. Diminished pain, less sputum, lower fever, a better bowel movement, or the rumbling of intestinal gas rewards the winners in the good fight. It is the absence of just that future-oriented attitude that helps make nursing homes the sad, depressing places they are—the absence of a hopeful tomorrow without an alternative mood that might give today some meaning.

Denial, too, is encouraged by the general atmosphere. Lord knows it is hard enough to see one sick person after another without being confronted with the grim honesty of failure, impatience, and helplessness. The flowers, the get-well cards, and bedside boxes of candy all urge not only resistance to, but denial of, fate and death. The patients, no matter how weak and sick, almost always answer the telephone the same way: "Better, thanks—doing pretty well." It is their duty to protect the rest of the world. All of us have social obligations, right down to the end.

The medical setting reinforces passivity, resistance, and denial (one at a time or in any combination) not only because things run more smoothly that way (sometimes I think that for the average medical administrator the ideal hospital would have no patients, just pieces of paper moving back and forth) but also because of the way we view disease. We tend to see the causes of death as impersonal forces, diseases whose causes in mechanistic terms leave little room for the active participation of the patient, except, that is, as resistance to death—fighting to get well—aids the doctor in his work. Even there, struggling for health is viewed not as the wondrous universal resource it is, but as the expected, the usual, the background, noted most in its absence, taken for granted the way we do the healing of a wound. As I noted earlier, in this view the patient is the arena over whose ground the doctor and his allies do battle with disease—the pot in which the surgeon plants his morning glory.

Even euthanasia, seemingly in the defense of the person, is spoken of in similar terms. One hears of passive euthanasia—letting death have its way—or active euthanasia—letting some merciful agency intervene.

This view of the role of the patient and of the disease is reinforced by the dominant mode of thought of our times, the rational analytic thought of science. That kind of thought has convinced us that the solutions to the problem of death lie outside of us, lie in things being done to us rather than coming from within us. I do not believe it necessary that science stop us at the border of the personal when we care for the dying, nor is it necessary for us to shed science when we enter the personal; they are both necessary and complementary views of our universe. Exemplifying the human condition, the problem of death has at its center the meeting of the universal and the intensely personal. And it would seem to me that the dying are best helped in the terms of the personal. The technological alternative, the banishment of death from life, has failed and we are thrown back on the human inner resources.

I believe that passivity, resistance, and denial are not the only postures in the face of death. There is another alternative. I think that it is possible for the physician to teach his patient how to die—to give his patient in this final stage of life the same kind of control that can be taught in earlier stages of living. When the patient has control over the process of dying, alleviation of pain and distress is possible and dying well becomes a meaningful and positive reality.

Control for the dying patient is not a simple matter, like taking a pill or a potion. Rather, control draws on the inner resources of the dying person, taps his innate ability to command the body, and then enlists the aid of those who surround him—family, friends, and physician. It is dependent on what humans have within themselves; to that extent it is a lonely thing, as is death itself. But the dying are also dependent on others, and that relationship is based on trust. Both inner resources and trust in others are required because the enemy of control is fear.

In order to understand how the dying are maintained in control and why that makes possible a better death, some insight into the fear of death is necessary. What is the age, who is the philosopher, and how many of us are there who have not given thought to the fear of death? It fills the fantasies of children and adolescents, occupies countless midnight hours of anxiety in the healthy, and infuses the contemplation of students of the human condition. Grown men mark themselves for their lifetimes on how well they have met that fear. Whole cultures and societies develop mechanisms to deny death and handle the fear of its omnipresence. Religions speak directly to the issue, and many people with a deeply held belief in God and the hereafter seem little afflicted by the fear of death. For them death is not an end but rather an entrance into a better world. I remember hearing with awe about an order of nuns that maintains an almost joyous watch at the bedside of a dying sister, a celebration of approaching union with God rather than sadness at an end. Most of us these days, however, are not so blessed—we have little confidence in our rebirth. Still, though, we wonder. When my mother died we had to tell my father, who was himself in the hospital, dying. After his initial shock and grief he said to us, "Now your mother knows something the rest of us only wonder about."

The Epicureans of classical Greece felt that one of the main functions of their philosophy was to free men from the fear of death without recourse to the intervention of the gods or a belief in an afterlife. Theirs was a philosophy of finitude.

From all of this we know that the fear of death is ubiquitous and that, considering the simple finality of its source, it should be easily understood. I think not, however, and some paradoxes point to its complexity. William Osler, the great physician, once wrote that he could hardly remember a dying patient who was afraid of death. That, too, has been my experience. In a recent study on the dying by Avery Weisman the same finding emerged; he concludes that the absence from his subjects of a fear of dying must be an artifact of observation, not a reliable indication of a lack of concern. But fear and concern are very different, and it would be an error to confuse the two. We certainly know within ourselves the difference between fear, where emotion is dominant, and concern, where content is dominant. For whatever reason, and leaving aside his interpretation of the data, his systematic findings confirm the common clinical experience that the fear of death is uncommon in the dying.

Another paradox presents itself. Generally speaking, the aged fear death very much less than the young. How odd it is that the closer one gets to death through the natural unfolding of years, the less frightening it becomes. The aged know death well. It has already taken from them many friends and those whom they loved. But no matter how much experience an old person may have had with the death of others, death remains the great unknown. The young have little experience with the presence of death and yet fear it greatly. (We have seen in an earlier chapter how important to the life of the young is their anxiety over death.) One may say in response to this that the older one gets, the less one cares about dying. While that may be true of the very old, we do not see older people leaping toward death "as onto a lover's couch." Rather, such a romantic expression of willingness to die is more a characteristic of the young, who are also much more ready to give their lives for a cause than the old are. It seems to be true that the aged care less about death.

It is an error to believe that not caring about death and wishing to die are the same. Equally, it is an error of psychological oversophistication to confuse the maturity implied in the loss of fear of dying with the psychological defense of denial. Who is denying what? It is not necessary to deny that which is no longer feared. When death becomes irrelevant, life has become no less dear. Life may be most meaningful in its present richness when death does not matter. But that may be seen as philosophical speculation, not relevant to our point, which concerns the care of the dying. In the service of that concern the meaning of the fear of death is most pertinent. It is not speculation, however, to repeat the paradox that those closest to death—the dying and the aged—fear death the least. That is what they say and that is how they behave. If you do not believe them or if you attribute the apparent lack of fear to some psychological mechanism or another, at least do not confuse the observation of the absence of a fear of death with your interpretation of its absence.

What is the fear of death? It is often said that the fear of death is the fear of the unknown. Did you fear the dark side of the moon before spaceships penetrated its mystery? It, too, was unknown. Do you fear the core of the earth, the cause of cancer, the life-force of viruses, the meaning of antimatter? They are all unknown but do not have meaning to each of us in the way that death has meaning to us. The very fact that unknown death has meaning to us separates its unknownness from things like Mars or viruses. That it has meaning suggests that we give substance to its mystery from within ourselves.

What within us provides the content of our fear? It has often been stated that no one can truly conceive of his own future nonexistence. Yet the dying do grieve over the loss of people whom they love and who will be lost to them solely because of their own deaths; that is to say, they are sad and mourn the loss of a child, for example, because of their own impending death, not the child's. In order to have such feelings, they must be able to think of their own absence. But mourning or grief is not fear. Is the fear fed by pictures of ourselves rotting in the ground, freezing in the grave, or turning to dust? We have no such pictures of ourselves, and it is constantly necessary to reiterate that those who know the most of the absolute fact of death seem to have the least fear. Furthermore, the fear of death appears in children so young (four or five) and so devoid of life experience as to cast doubt that the fear is of the unknown, future nonexistence, or the body rotting in the grave.

What, then, is the fear of death? In the child it is the fear of nothingness, the fear of separation and disappearance, the fear of the loss of object or separation from object. All these fears have their basis in reality. The child has been nothing. The child has known separation and disappearance because in normal growth it must separate and differentiate itself from the parent. Further, as I pointed out before, infants and very young children do not seem to distinguish between mind and body. There is no separate existence of the mind. What is vanished from sight is lost—and almost all of this is beyond the control of the infant. In its growth from complete identity with parent and environment the child loses the oceanic feeling of infancy, the glorious oneness with self and the world. But both the feeling and the loss are remembered. It has been said that the night terrors of childhood are a memory and re-creation of those physical separations, a replay of the dangers of disappearance and nothingness. The stimulus that engenders the terror is physical. The reaction to the stimulus is both physical and emotional. Terror, despair, and fear are feelings represented in both mind and body. The memory of how death is represented in the mind and body is thus always at hand, providing the trigger to set off the fear of death whether a body part is threatened or the loss of a relationship is at hand.

Commonly associated with the fear of death are fears of various kinds of illness. The body is seen as a betrayer, not to be trusted, an unsure and unsafe place in which to be. Pushed to the extremity of her fears, one patient, a woman in her forties plagued by body fears but otherwise happy and happily married, with a good and fulfilling job and happy, healthy children, felt her body as the enemy slipping back toward nothingness, helpless and out of control. Helplessness and the loss of control so characteristic of infancy lay at the center of her fears. Deep within was the memory of total dependency on the other, an untrustworthy other because of the helplessness of infancy. So much did the memory remain that any situation in which things seemed too much to cope with, in which chaos or helplessness threatened, would elicit fear—fear of sickness, fear of cancer, fear of death. Experience suggests that she is not alone, that the fear of death has at its roots in many of us the fear of the loss of control and the fear of utter helplessness.

Is it not possible, then, that we, the living, remote from our own deaths but standing at the bedside of the dying, have confused our own fear of death with their fear of dying and in that confusion have denied our dying patients a means to remain in control of their own deaths? The core of our fears is buried in our minds and bodies and closed to us, but we attribute to the patient the same fear. Our fear is a luxury of the healthy and the living, an abstraction of our past. The sick deal with the concrete —pain, nausea, thirst, weakness, the fear that they won't be able to "take it," and so on. Those are the things that form the basis of the fears of the dying, and with good reason. They do not constitute the fear of death but rather the fear of the messy details and the burdens of dying. We hide from the painful memory of our past and the mystery of the future, but their pain is in the present. Our silence contains the battle within us between the force that drives us to live and to function and the desire to return to an oceanic peace. To the patient that inner war has become a wasteful extravagance causing only pain in the face of a determined fate. Our silence in the presence of the dying, seemingly necessary to us, denies the dying patient the means with which to die well. In practical terms all of this means that it is possible to help the dying patient in a most concrete and positive manner, to assist him to die in relative comfort, in control of himself and his body, or, alternatively, to live as long as possible in the manner of the living, not chained to his impending death.

We spend our lives fighting sickness, regression, disability, and death. Physicians spend their lives in the service of that fight, exhorting and abetting the will to live, the life-force. Call it what you will, measurable or not, we know that the life-force exists and that it is potent. But there is a time to stop—not merely to stop the application of technology but to actively help the dying patient develop the will to die.

This can be done with the very ill and the aged, in the most practical terms. It is possible to suggest to the patient that the time has come to leave, but at the same time it is necessary to reassure him that it is all right to leave and that it is not going to hurt. We are all afraid of unknown pain, but things rarely hurt as much as we thought they were going to. When this is explained to a patient, the doctor is amazed to discover that the patient becomes more peaceful; that pain, if present, becomes less severe and more bearable; and that within a relatively short time the patient dies.

A seventy-eight-year-old woman had a biopsy diagnosis of cancer of the esophagus made three months before the first time I saw her. She had received appropriate cobalt radiation and remained essentially free of symptoms for about two months. At that time she began to have increasing pain and inability to swallow and an X ray was interpreted as showing a tracheoesophageal fistula (a hole in the esophagus—a dire complication). When she was admitted to the hospital she did not have the appearance of a dying person, but our X rays, while they did not confirm the fistula, revealed the far-advanced state of her disease. All she could expect was ever-increasing pain and gradual starvation.

She had been told little else other than that she had a tumor. Consultation with surgeons and other physicians supported the conclusion that there was virtually nothing to offer that would do more than briefly prolong her life—a painful life at that. The family, stating that she had always been a strong-willed, independent, and dignified person, was against any life-prolonging heroics. All this was noted on the chart.

I had a long conversation with the patient. I said that I could do nothing further for her tumor, which would continue to grow. However, most of my statement was positive; she was told that she had much more power over her own body than she knew and that I would support her in whatever she decided to do. I made it clear that there was nothing to be frightened of, that everything would be done to make sure that she had as little pain or distress as possible. Three aspects were emphasized: the disease could not be cured; she had more control over the situation than she knew and would be supported in whatever course she decided to follow; she was not to be frightened, because pain and distress could and would be controlled. The following day she said, "I guess you said I have to learn to live with it." I agreed and again emphasized the amount of control she had and told her that she should not be afraid of pain.

The next day she developed a fever. Eight days later she died of untreated pneumococcal septicemia. Throughout her brief terminal illness she was quite comfortable, requiring less medication for pain than expected. On each visit, support and freedom from fear and pain were underlined. No hope of cure was extended but, curiously, hope itself was maintained. Our relation seemed good. In the last few days her consciousness became clouded and she died in a coma.

It must be emphasized that the psychological pattern that was developed in the care of this woman was very different from that ordinarily provided. Although her impending death and cancer were not specifically discussed, I did not exhort her to "fight" or get better and did not discuss the future. Emphasis on getting better and on the future are so much a part of the usual framework of medical care that they have become invisible. Consciously changing the mental pattern is difficult, since every word and action must be monitored.

Changing the pattern is the equivalent of changing the most basic rules of treatment. Doing this is hard on the physician. The process strikes deep within and elicits painful resonance in the doctor. It is difficult to find the proper words, and yet absolute honesty is required. The doctor must openly face his responsibility. He must be sure, in the light of his knowledge and judgment, that indeed the time has come for the patient to leave.

Sometimes teaching the aged how to die turns into teaching the dying how to live. An attorney in his seventies had his first operation for cancer of the larynx a few years before I first cared for him. A number of other operations had been necessary in the intervening period to deal with local recurrence of the disease and to correct problems that arose from the way in which he neglected his tracheostomy. He had not learned to talk following his surgery, and one of the first necessary steps was to persevere past his stubbornness and frustration in order to teach him how to use the voice machine. My part of his case was the control of his heart disease and the thyroid and parathyroid complications arising from the previous radical surgery. He was irascible, careless with the numerous medicines he required, and difficult to deal with.

One day he and his son came into the office unannounced. The patient looked terrible—frightened and sick. The son, in his early thirties, was also obviously shaken. They had been to the doctors who had done his surgery, since he had developed a regrowth of the cancer in the back of his throat and swallowing was troublesome. The surgeons told him that there was no more that could be done for him. Chemotherapy was suggested, but the physicians were frank in explaining that it was little more than a placebo.

My conversation was straightforward. I asked him what he was so frightened by—death? No, he wasn't afraid of dying. He wrote his replies because it was no longer possible for him to speak, even with the machine. I suggested that the problem was that he was being dragged around by his disease, as though, when there was nothing to be done for his cancer, there was nothing to be done for him. There was much that could and would be done. Was he afraid of pain? I would teach him in the greatest detail how pain was controlled and give him every necessary tool for its control. Did he not want to go to the hospital? Why should he, since everything that was necessary could be done at home? Even nursing, should it become necessary, could be arranged. If his food was prepared with a blender and some imagination, he would be able to swallow nourishment more easily than up until now and swallowing would certainly be easier if he stopped struggling. Step by step we went over the problems, with practical concrete solutions offered to each one. He was told again that he had much more control over his body than he had any idea. Fear was the enemy.

The son was in despair at the conversation, but the patient became calm. I never saw him again but continued to run the case by telephone and in conversations with his most helpful wife. From time to time it was necessary to reinforce the process and calm fears with specific treatment suggestions. About one year later some tumor mass was removed by cryosurgery. Death occurred eighteen months later after a brief terminal coma. I was amazed at the length of survival. I was even more amazed at the change in him reported by his family. He was much easier to live with, more open. His wife wrote to me after his death, "Allen died Wednesday evening about 10 o'clock. He went quietly and peacefully out of his 'semicoma' after a quiet day in which I often sat beside him for an hour or so and let him grasp my hand hard with his left hand—the only communicative part that was left. Your counsel meant a great deal to me and enabled me to let him go in peace. You helped Bob [the son] stop trying to rescue him, too, and both of us have come out of it well."

A businessman in his sixties had been operated on for cancer of the large intestine two years before I first saw him. While on a business trip to another city he developed an intestinal blockage and emergency surgery was performed. He was found to have recurrent cancer with small areas of disease scattered throughout the abdomen. The family told me that he did not know his diagnosis and did not want to know.

He recovered rapidly after his operation and was soon back at work. He was somewhat fearful about his illness and, although closemouthed, read into every symptom a return of disability. However, he was urged to get on with his work and life. On a routine visit about four months after his operation, although he was feeling well, I discovered a large mass within the abdomen. Two weeks later he returned because of abdominal pain. The mass had grown so large in those two weeks that it now almost filled the abdomen. It was clear that his cancer had spread rapidly and widely. No meaningful treatment was availble to halt his disease. In the consulting room after his examination his silence made conversation difficult. "You're in trouble," I said; "you're in real trouble." I explained that he could go back to work as long as possible or enter the hospital. He needn't worry about pain or sickness because I could and would keep him free from distress. He went home, but in a day or so called and asked to be admitted to the hospital. In the hospital his disease progressed extremely rapidly and he had partial intestinal obstruction throughout his hospital days. Consultations with surgeons and other physicians and a review of the pathology slides from the previous recent operation confirmed the view that any treatment or further surgery would be pointless. Instead of the pain and misery usually associated with intestinal obstruction, he was amazingly free of discomfort and required only minimal medication.

Because he was so taciturn, and because both the facts of his disease and of his impending death were unspoken, talking to him was difficult for me. Nonetheless, the theme of his control over his body and the importance of his not becoming frightened because all the details could be handled was emphasized again and again. This reassurance was often given in reference to such matters as taking fluids or comfortable positions in the bed, since the larger issues seemed closed to conversation. I am more skilled now than I was then and I wonder whether I could now be more direct. However, the instance shows that we are often just as able to convey meaning by metaphor or indirection as by directness.

The family, especially the children, urged that more be done, and he was scheduled for surgery two days hence. He died the night before the operation, two weeks after our initial conversation.

A woman in her early fifties was operated on for a cancer of the stomach. She remained entirely well for four years and then developed abdominal symptoms. Tests and X rays showed recurrence of the cancer with a complication: gastrocolic fistula (an abnormal connection between the stomach and the colon) that required surgery for the relief of her symptoms. The operation revealed the widespread nature of her cancer. She knew her diagnosis at the time of her first operation, but her husband felt that she should not be told the seriousness of her present situation.

Every time I went into her room I felt the discomfort of unspoken words. I finally said to her that I wasn't afraid of words like "death" or "cancer" and that she could speak to me about those things, since her husband could not bear the pain of the conversation. As in the other case, I told her about the extent of her control and how the enemy of that control was fear. She was given chronic chemotherapy (5-fluorouracil), although it was made clear to her husband that the treatment offered little hope. Her husband wanted every extra minute of life that could be gained and often sent me newspaper clippings or other information about cancer cures. I faithfully followed up each lead. It seemed to me that I was obligated both to her desire that she be comfortable and that the whole thing not last too long and to his wish that every possible useful thing be done to prolong life.

Months went by and on each visit she was told in explicit detail how to control each symptom. Sometimes hot packs to her abdomen and sometimes cold packs brought comfort. She didn't like the dulling of her thoughts that narcotics produced, and so small, frequent doses of various medications were used, often in combination to produce the greatest relief with the fewest side effects. Again, she was remarkably free from pain, although weakness—one symptom that I could not, and never can, control—troubled her. In the last few days of her life her pain increased, and she and I agreed that the time had come for large doses of pain medication. We had kept our pact of conversation about her illness that allowed her to be silent with her family on the subject. In death, as in life, the relationship between our private self and the self that belongs to others is very complex and delicate. I would have wished, in caring for her, that honest, loving, but conflicting desires of husband and wife did not both have to be met. But the care of the dying, as of the living, should take place within, and not override, the framework of the person's life (except in special circumstances and for short periods).

For many years I knew and admired Catherine Morrissey, a nurse in a hospital that I used. She really knew how to take care of sick people, and the doctor who didn't listen to what she told him about his patients was a fool. From a working-class background, she was one of those women meant by the words "a pillar of strength." She raised many children and saw them become lawyers, physicians, and successful businessmen. After I had left that hospital I was asked to see her in consultation; she had had a diagnosis of cancer of the jaw. She told me that she liked the way I cared for dying patients and made me promise that if it came to that I wouldn't let her suffer.

Two years passed without a word from her, and then one day I received a desperate call from one of her daughters-in-law. Could I admit Mrs. Morrissey to the hospital because she was in poor shape? The case had gone badly and in the past months she felt that she had been virtually abandoned by her doctor. I was shocked when I saw her. The "pillar of strength" had been replaced by an agonized, trembling, pitifully frightened, crying creature. The side of her face was occupied by draining abscesses and open, infected wounds. She could hardly talk or swallow. Before doing anything else, I gave her large doses of morphine and Thorazine to control her pain, nausea, and agitation. I wanted her to know instantly that I would keep my promise and that pain control was possible. It took several days of tests and consultations to determine whether her state was caused by cancer, hopelessness, or infection. If it were only the latter two, she could be returned to her life. Unfortunately, the basic problem was uncontrollable cancer.

In the few days occupied in making a definitive diagnosis, she was kept free of pain and her "cool" returned. We discussed her impending death and her potential control over the process. I explained to her that if she wanted to die now, she could. It wouldn't take very long—perhaps two weeks. It was necessary only that it be her sincere wish and that she remain free of fear. She was more direct in her words than any previous patient with whom I had dealt. She made me wonder whether the absence of directness in the past had come from the patients or from my hesitancy. In any case she was doubtful as to whether her death would come about so soon simply because she wished it. I assured her that it would. Experience had taught me that this strange phenomenon, which I did not understand, was quite reliable. Again I was explicit about the details of medication, diet, wound care, and so forth. The pain that had previously required so much medication became minor, requiring only small and infrequent doses of narcotics. Calm descended over her room. The family gathered as in the old-fashioned descriptions of a dying parent. One of the floor nurses asked me why the family was so tranquil, and I said, having by this time quite regularly observed this, that it was because the patient was calm and free of fear.

Once, on making my rounds, I found her crying. She was, she told me, sad to be losing them all. A few days before she died she said, "Doctor, what is my prognosis?" An odd question, since she knew the whole story. "No," she said, "I mean how many days?" The words shot through me, causing a sharp inward wince. "Only a few more days, Catherine."

It has taken me a long time to get used to those conversations. From the beginning when they were so painful to me that I could hardly get the words out of my mouth, I had felt that with time I would get over my distress. In an odd way I thought that getting over the fears and distress associated with dealing directly with death would be like dealing with the sexual feelings associated with patients that I had learned to cope with many years earlier. The feelings that went with death, just like the sexual feelings, would stop troubling me if I dealt with them directly instead of trying to pretend that they were not there!

Two more brief cases to make two more points. A sixty-nine-year-old woman was operated on for cancer of the large intestine, which was found to be extensive and incurable. Before the operation she told her surgeon, and me, that whatever happened she wanted to be told the truth. Her husband had died about a year and a half earlier without ever having been told, and that had been extremely distressing to her. Three days after surgery I found her deeply depressed. The surgeon had been truthful with her. All doctors are familiar with the scene and have learned to expect the consequences. The patient wants honesty but in its trail come depression, long and slow postoperative recovery, more severe or prolonged pain than following surgery for nonfatal disease. That sad picture is one of the reasons physicians often try to avoid honesty.

"What are you so sad about?" I said. "Who wouldn't be upset after hearing what I did?" she answered. I said, "Are you afraid of dying? You already told me that you haven't cared whether you live or die since your husband passed away. Are you afraid of pain or of being a burden on your son?" She began to cry. I went on. "Except for weakness, Helen, there is almost no symptom you can have that I cannot teach you to control. I will show you what to do and how to do it, including giving yourself injections, if necessary." She made a face. "It will be easier than you think, I promise you. You are going to remain in control and you will not be helpless as long as you don't get frightened. We don't know how long you are going to live any more than you knew before this operation. However long it is, you will have the tools and the knowledge to remain the person you are. When it comes time to die, it won't take long and even that will be under your control.

If by being a burden you mean that you will need your son's help, you are right. But I don't think that is what you mean. When you say burden you mean 'helpless burden' and that is not going to happen."

The conversation continued, covering more details about all the problems that might come up. By the next day the change in her was remarkable. She made an extremely rapid recovery. She is still alive. Her son says that she tells him she is sure the doctors are all wrong, but anyway it doesn't matter. When I see her, she gets an anxious look as she brings up the subject of pain, but it goes away as we discuss how to use the virtual drugstore I have provided, should the medicines become necessary.

As I write this chapter I have another patient in the hospital dying from cancer of the pancreas. He is an old man whose family told me that I must not tell him his diagnosis. That would be impossible. He has been sick for eight months, losing weight and in pain, as endless diagnostic tests failed to reveal the cause. At last he was transferred to my care and we found the source, confirmed at operation. His brother had died of cancer of the pancreas, the same disease we found in him. How could I not tell him without his thinking that I was not trustworthy and without his fears being compounded by the silence? I assured the family that he would do remarkably well and would probably decide to die. Judging from his life, I believed he would probably do that well also.

Yesterday I visited his room, along with two medical students. They listened as he and I spoke about the details of his dying and as I assured him that it wouldn't take long. When we left his bedside they were literally dumbstruck. They had never heard a conversation like that and were amazed at how straightforward and simple it all seemed. They were equally amazed at how comfortable and calm the patient was and how calm and accepting his family was, as they were there also. The students said that they had never seen anything like it. I understood their reaction because before I dealt with dying patients in this manner, I, too, had never seen anything like it. But it certainly is a better way.

Later, one of the students asked me what the patient was dying from. I didn't know, but I did know that cancer of the pancreas would not be an honest or complete answer. I do not understand the phenomenon but I have come to trust it. In medicine we are forever dealing with natural forces, with things in the body we do not understand. But with caution, experience, and discipline we learn to use these things for the benefit of our patients.

I should like to reiterate the basic points of the approach. At the time a patient is given the bad news, he is also told how much control over the situation he has. I actually use the words, "You have more control over your body than you have any idea." I point out that the enemy of his control is fear. I then try to find out exactly what he is afraid of in the greatest detail. As pointed out earlier, the fears always turn out to be concrete. In equal and explicit detail I show how each problem can be, or will be, handled. I do my best to be absolutely honest, since I am sure it would be quickly apparent if I dissembled. Honesty here is rarely difficult, inasmuch as misconceptions about the disease, drugs, or dying make up a large number of the fears. On questions I cannot answer, such as "How long will I live?" I am also honest, but I often point out how much of the outcome is within the patient's power. Having promised the control of the symptoms or situations, it is absolutely essential that the promise be upheld.

This often requires considerable flexibility in the use of medications, telephone calls, visits, and so forth. In the hospital it also requires the cooperation of nurses and house staff. The nursing staff usually welcomes the approach, but the residents and interns require more support. However, the innovative care of the dying finds a more receptive climate among young physicians these days.

Since in the terminally ill what is being done is tantamount to telling the patient to die, one must have the technical or clinical evidence as well as consultations where indicated to support that judgment. The doctor must openly face his responsibility. He must be certain, in the light of medical science and his own experience and judgment, that indeed the time has come for the patient to leave.

The process is based on trust. The patient is being told that it is permissible, indeed necessary, to stop doing something that he has done his whole life—namely, battling for life—and he is being told that it will not hurt. To accept that assurance requires a deep trust of one human for another.

The physician's ability to help the patient die comes not only from his eliciting the patient's trust but from a part of his general function: the giving of permission. The social scientists, who have pointed out that physicians validate their patients' illnesses for society, fail to see the constant battle between self and body, between pain and will, that takes place in illness. The disease may be the cause and the social setting may be the stage, but the battle is in the person. It is the physician who gives permission for a person who becomes ill to stop and do battle for his body. And, once health has returned, it is the physician who gives permission to get on with life once again without fear of or for the body. In the case of the dying, the physician can, based on trust and the service of his patient, give permission for the person to stop the battle for life.

The process of care that I have described has evolved over several years. In the beginning it was extremely difficult and painful for me. Finding words was always troublesome and I would get physical symptoms (the same back pain that occurred when my parents died would recur each time I had to deal with one of these patients). With increasing experience it has become easier. My words are more straightforward and simple and I am more sensitive to the process. The same problems have occurred so often that I have acquired greater facility in dealing with them. Increasingly, I have applied the same principles to the care of other chronic problems such as heart disease, arthritis, or diabetes. There seems to me nothing new in all this. Dying patients have done it on their own probably since the beginning of time. It requires that physicians and medicine not get in the way but rather facilitate the process. I think that others, using their own words and manner, will, if they are patient with their learning, find it equally gratifying.

The cases I have cited are all successes. Naturally there are also failures. Where denial is very strong, I feel no obligation to breach it; indeed, I believe that denial should be supported where it constitutes the patient's main defense.

Other patients' body fears are so rooted that I cannot overcome them. I seem unable to give them the sense of riding their body toward good or ill, or the control of their physical being that is at the root of this concept. In a recent book about his leukemia, *Stay of Execution*, Stewart Alsop describes a situation terribly common today. He is inexorably tied to his platelet count and his bone marrow findings. If his checkup shows that his platelet count is good, he is exalted; if the count is bad, he is thrown into a depression. This is a perfect example of a patient being dragged around by his disease and out of control. We understand his pleasure at the news that he will live longer. It is terrible, however, when the sick person confuses himself with his platelet count, a confusion too frequently fostered by the physicians. Things can go well and the patient remain in control, but they can go badly and still the patient need not feel helpless. Living or dying, he remains himself. Dying is unimportant. It is not that it doesn't matter; it does, but it is unimportant. What is important is that he remains intact, fully functioning as a person to the extent possible until he dies. A patient who is constantly fearful about his platelet count, the water in his ankles, or the growth of his tumor cannot remain intact. He will be constantly at the mercy of his fears and of his body—in other words, helpless.

I have few such patients, however. Most can be given back their sense of control. They will be sad on hearing bad news, but not depressed deeply or for very long. After all, it is sad to die, but it is inevitable.

All the examples cited have been older people with cancer. I am an internist and so have little experience with the death of the young. What experience I have suggests that young people can be trained to have the same sense of control as the aged. The problem is to teach them how to live their lives as fully as possible to the very end. The tools are the same. In nonmalignant disease the prediction of outcome is more difficult but the same principles apply. Where senility or dementia is present, it seems impossible for the patient to remain in control sufficiently to die when he wishes or to continue to function well. Perhaps the greatest tragedy is the patient whose mental functions are so impaired that teaching is impossible, but whose disease, such as heart disease or stroke, will allow a prolonged life. Sometimes, however, the seemingly senile who are given back some control over their state return to excellent mental function.

What I have described in the care of the dying applies equally well to the care of the living. It is not a trick that works for the dying, but rather an approach to the sick, some of whom live and some of whom die. That a man dies of an incurable disease may represent a failure of medical science, but that does not need to mean failure for an individual physician. Medical science strives to push back the borders of the unknown, but physicians care for the sick, employing that science as far as it can give benefit and using themselves as the treatment modality when the remedies of science are exhausted.

It should be apparent that the attitude of control toward death that has been portrayed in such detail is different from the attitudes of passivity, resistance, or denial. But one might ask why this is not simply resignation or acceptance of death. I think that there is a difference. Both acceptance and resignation are passive concepts. These patients have accepted death and are resigned to its inevitability, but that is only a step on their road. Theirs is a more active stance; they are doing something. They are not merely awaiting the arrival of death, calm as they may be; rather, they seem to make it part of their living. The ones who die quickly appear to make a partner of death in their orderly retreat from the world. The others who go on to longer life seem somehow to have no sense of death pulling at them, as though they had risen above time.

My own view is that the process derives from a greater unity of person and body than is usual in our culture, reminding one of the classic Greek attitude. We are a society that in many ways has discarded the body except as transportation for the head or as a provider for some pleasant sensations on which the mind can operate.

There are, in recent times, signs of a return to an understanding of the body's place in human completeness. Esalen, transcendental meditation, the popularity of Eastern religions (albeit in a somewhat instant-hip fashion), and other signs all point to the reemergence of a more evenly balanced mind-body construct. While one might wish for somewhat less ideology in each of these expressions of the trend (it *is* possible to eat a balanced diet without facing east in the process), the growing awareness that mind and body should exist in harmony is encouraging. An attempt to understand the meaning of the body in man's life occupies a number of recent writings. Ernest Becker in *The Denial of Death* views the essential paradox of life as unresolvable. The conflict is between the transcendent mind and the frail body so liable to putrefaction. He cannot find a solution other than a return to faith because the body cannot be denied its final say—death—and the great religions in which the problem of the body's evanescence is solved by life after death have failed us. Norman O. Brown, in *Life Against Death*, also urges us to resurrect the body. What the world needs "is a little more Eros and less strife." But, after pleading that the body be allowed to be more than just an anchor, he seems to say that the function of the Eros is to add a little spice to the intellect. No resolution of the paradox, just more joy. One cannot fault more joy, but neither Becker nor Brown nor others involved in the back-to-the-body movement seem to ring true alongside the phenomena of the dying patients I have described.

As man emerges from infancy, he must transcend his body in order to grow. And then, when he is somewhat older, he must ride it as surely as the cowboy rides his horse, knowing that its limits are his limits. But what of later? Is the body still only useful as a vehicle or a source of pleasant sensations? I think that those who die well and in control have something to teach the living about the body and about living. They show us that it is possible to come to peace with the body, both to be controlled by its limitations and to control it to a far greater extent than unlearned existence would suggest. They teach us that control is not denial or repression. That which we deny or repress about ourselves or within ourselves controls us by the very fact of our constant need to deny rather than to come to terms. Control implies acceptance of limitations plus an awareness that the limitations provide room for the continued exercise of self, even unto death. The beauty and potential of growth lie not only in intellectual transcendence and the formation of transcendent emotional bonds, but also in the possibility of dynamic unity with the body. In that state the fear of death, an essentially backward look, becomes unimportant.

Perhaps a story will best serve to convey my sense of how these patients rise above their fear of death—to show that more is involved than mere acceptance or resignation. It is the story told by Konrad Ferdinand Meyer, a nineteenth-century Swiss poet and novelist little known to readers of English, in his historical novel *The Temptation of Pescara.*

In the early sixteenth century Pescara was a powerful and successful general, who commanded the Spanish forces in Italy for the Emperor of Spain. At that time control of the Italian city-states was being fought for by the French, German, and Spanish princes against the disarrayed armies of the Pope. Feared and respected by his enemies for his military brilliance, Pescara had won the decisive battle of Pavia in 1525, during which he was seriously wounded.

The novel opens with Pescara's determination, despite his wound, to lead his army against Milan, the next prize he will offer the Spanish Emperor. Anticipation of this battle sparks endless intrigue among the princes of the city-states and the Pope to avoid the fall of Milan. In this setting of treason and corruption, Morone, the chancellor to the Duke of Milan, attempts to persuade Pescara to desert the Spanish and lead the Italian forces in expelling the invaders from Italy. To tempt Pescara to betray his emperor, Morone offers him the throne of a new nation to be formed of the city-states, since Morone is sure that no man could refuse such glory.

But Pescara is beyond temptation. Unknown to anyone but himself and his physician, he is dying of his wound. He listens to Morone but rejects his proposal, despite the entreaties of his wife, who tries to convince him to accept the offer.

Italy is not ready, he feels, for liberty. Freedom is not born out of treason and betrayal. Saddened by the brutal excesses of the Spanish in their conquests (including the murder of his father), it is not out of loyalty to the emperor that he turns aside the proffered glory. What makes him reject treason is loyalty to himself as a man.

Pescara proceeds with his military plans to conquer Milan. Before the battle he visits a church and approaches the figure of Christ as an equal, not out of arrogance but with the humility of his imminent death.

The battle is won and Milan is taken. He offers humane concessions to protect the Duke of Milan, thus causing his Spanish aides to suspect him of treason. But despite their threats and the corruption around him he is steadfast in his integrity. He dies while trying to bind the Emperor to his own benevolent commitments.

In Pescara we see a man who, freed of the fear of death, rises above the temptations of glory and immortality. To the dying who no longer fear death, such things are irrelevant. It is the fear of death, not death itself, that keeps men incomplete, thus driving them to seek immortality.

"Medicine," Hippocrates said, "is more necessary to philosophy than philosophy is to medicine." Nature continually drives men to form theories that might give order to nature. But nature is not guided by the theories of men. For the physician, nature is portrayed in the sick. Our theories and constructs about sickness and disease have come and gone through the ages, but the sick have remained essentially the same. It is to them that the physician owes his allegiance and, ultimately, it is in them that the truth resides.

Selected Bibliography

Ackerknecht, Erwin H. *Medicine and Ethnology: Selected Essays.* Edited by H. H. Walser and H. M. Koebing. Baltimore: The Johns Hopkins Press, 1971.

Cassell, Eric J. "Death and the Physician." *Commentary,* Vol. 47, No. 6 (June 1969), pp. 73–79.

———. "Disease as a Way of Life." *Commentary,* Vol. 55 (February 1973), pp. 80–82.

———. "Dying in a Technological Society." The Hastings Center Studies, Vol. 2 (May 1974), pp. 31–36.

———. "In Sickness and in Health." *Commentary,* Vol. 49, No. 6 (June 1970), pp. 59–66.

———. "Learning to Die." Bulletin of the New York Academy of Medicine, Second Series, Vol. 49 (December 1973), pp. 1110–1118.

———. "Making and Escaping Moral Decisions." The Hastings Center Studies, Vol. 1 (1973), pp. 53–62.

———. "On Educational Changes for the Field of Aging." *The Gerontologist,* Vol. 12 (1972), pp. 251–256.

———. "Permission to Die." *Bioscience,* Vol. 23 (August 1973), pp. 475–477.

———. "Preliminary Explorations of Thinking in Medicine." *Ethics in Science and Medicine,* Vol. 2 (1975), pp. 1–12.

————. "Treating the Dying—The Doctor vs. The Man Within The Doctor." *Medical Dimensions,* Vol. 1, no. 1 (1972), pp. 6–11, 22.

Deuschle, Kurt, and Adair, John. "An Interdisciplinary Approach to Public Health on the Navaho Indian Reservation: Medical and Anthropological Aspects." Annals of the New York Academy of Sciences, Vol. 84 (1960), pp. 887–905.

Engelhardt, H. Tristram, Jr. "The Concepts of Health and Disease." In *Evaluation and Explanation in the Biomedical Sciences,* edited by H. Tristram Engelhardt, Jr., and Stuart F. Spicker. Dordrecht, Holland: D. Reidel Publishing Company, forthcoming.

Hall, Edward T. *The Hidden Dimension.* New York: Doubleday & Company, Inc., 1966.

Hippocrates. *The Genuine Works of Hippocrates.* Translated by Francis Adams. New York: William Wood and Company, 1886.

Lain Entralgo, Pedro. *Doctor and Patient.* Translated by Frances Partridge. New York, Toronto: World University Library, McGraw Hill Book Co., 1969.

————. *The Therapy of the Word in Classical Antiquity.* Edited and translated by L. J. Rather and John M. Sharp. New Haven, London: Yale University Press, 1970.

Lévi-Strauss, Claude. *Structural Anthropology.* Garden City, New York: Anchor Books, Doubleday & Company, Inc., 1967.

McDermott, Walsh. "Environmental Factors Bearing on Medical Education in the Developing Countries:

Manpower for the World's Health." Association of American Medical Colleges, 1966.

————, Deuschle, Kurt, and Barnett, C. "Health Care Experiment at Many Farms." *Science*, Vol. 175 (1972), pp. 23–31.

Winkelstein, Warren. "Epidemiological Considerations Underlying the Allocation of Health and Disease Care Resources." *International Journal of Epidemiology*, Vol. I (1972), pp. 69–74.

Index